By the same author

BLUE GUIDE: ROMANIA
(A & C Black)

LES ORIENTALISTES DE L'ÉCOLE ITALIENNE
(ACR Edition)

Caroline Juler

Searching
for
Sarmizegetusa

Journeys to the heart of rural Romania

with a foreword by
Jessica Douglas-Home

———

Starborn Books

SEARCHING FOR SARMIZEGETUSA

Caroline Juler

First published in 2003
by Starborn Books
Glanrhydwilym, Rhydwilym,
Clunderwen, Pembs.,
Wales, U.K.

Text and all illustrations including
cover photograph © Caroline Juler 2002
Music examples pp. 64 & 90 © Lucy Castle 2003

Cover photograph, drawings and maps by Caroline Juler
Music examples by Lucy Castle

ISBN   1 899530 11 8

Contents

Drawings and Maps

Foreword
by
Jessica Douglas-Home

For nearly two hundred years, a small but continuous trickle of English men and women have travelled through Central and Eastern Europe, immersing themselves in the many-patterned cultures of Poland, Czechoslovakia, Hungary and the Balkans.

To many of these travellers, Romania has exerted the most powerful fascination. They have found that this country more than any other has illuminated their inner beliefs with the intensity of a magnifying glass. So it has been for Caroline Juler, whose quest in 2003 is entangled in a riddle. On the one hand, she hopes to maintain the beauty and mythology of a country whose way of life, still similar to that of the pre-Industrialised England of her forefathers, hangs by a thread. On the other hand has she the right, she asks herself, to seek to impose restraints on the process of modernisation, to deprive those who live in poverty from acquiring telephones, television sets, black leather sofas and internal sanitation, which many assume to be basic necessities of life?

Nowhere is this dilemma more acute than in Saxon Transylvania. Until very recently the German-speaking Romanian community there was 250,000 strong, having established itself during eight centuries in two hundred villages and seven towns just north of the southern Carpathians. Ensconced among Hungarians and Romanians, and threatened over the centuries by the Turks and Tartars, the Saxons never surrendered their distinctive way of life and ancient traditions.

Their villages are some of the most beautiful and unspoilt in Europe, displaying a remarkable harmony between people and landscape. No modern buildings blight the original medieval layout: ducks and geese wander freely in untarmacked cobbled streets where cattle leave each morning and return each night to their own separate courtyards; the solid one-storey houses sit end on to the street, washed in blue, green, terracotta, or golden ochre yellow, with steep hipped roofs and pretty decorative stucco work. To one side of the house a large wooden gate will enter onto a cobbled courtyard, winter and summer kitchens, a vegetable patch and colossal timber frame barn enclosing the rear end of the courtyard. A wide stream runs down the street between an alley of pear trees.

In the centre of many of the villages stands a vast medieval fortified church. In times of siege the villagers would move inside

7

the walls, sometimes three rings thick, where each family had a room with a store of food and even a school for the children. Inside, the churches are calm and peaceful, the galleries and side pews charmingly decorated, painted with delicate designs of flowers, trees, birds or primitive views of villages. Extraordinary 15th century altarpieces match those of Renaissance Italy. Now none but a few of the old Saxon families remain, guarding this ancient and fascinating culture.

Soon after Ceausescu was shot in December 1989, the German government invited anyone of German origin to return to the Fatherland. Life had been hard under Communism. Grasping at the chance, the Saxons laid down their sickles, sold their horses and carts, boarded up their houses and emigrated en bloc.

But all is not lost. During the last three years resourceful remaining Saxons have been involved in a project to promote, restore and conserve the Saxon villages. Their aim is to keep this crumbling legacy for future generations. Besides repairing facades and stucco work and barns and churches, they have started up guest houses. Tourists with a sense of adventure are flocking to the area - Romanians from Bucharest, visitors from France, England and Germany. They discover a region characterised by vast tracts of land with ancient cart tracks running through forests roamed by lynx, wolves and bear into valleys and villages abundant with wild flowers now all but extinct in Western Europe.

Communities elsewhere in Romania should take heart - and so perhaps should Caroline Juler. Here in Transylvania there are indeed TVs and sanitation, mobile telephones and simple comfortable furniture. But the spirit and fabric of an ancient world survives alongside the modern amenities, kept alive for a new generation of villagers and for visitors, maybe learning of the opportunities from the internet, who want to travel back in time.

Jessica Douglas-Home, February 2003

THANKS

Having spent six years preparing the Romanian Blue Guide, it has been a relief to write this one within six months. Peter Oram has been that rare combination of a sympathetic and meticulous editor. Lots of other people have lent a hand and there is space to mention a few: Ramona Gönczöl and Cristina Rai for their instant translations, Lucy Castle for musical notation and song lyrics, Ioana Cataniciu for her view of the communist period, Parasca Fat for explaining previously unpublished details of Maramureş mythology, and the Iuga family who provided technical aid, encouragement and rapid answers to no doubt tedious questions. Kit deserves a medal for his writer's support service. Last but not least, I have to report that Betsy, our beloved Sherpa van, has been sent to the retirement home at Glandy Cross. She gave lifts to scores of Romanians and once brought me safe and sound all the way from Cluj to Crymych without a starter motor.

To Horia, Dana and Brânduşa

Searching
for
Sarmizegetusa

Why Sarmizegetusa?

Ulmu-mi este verişor,
Iar stejarul frăiţior,
Că la vreme şi la zor
Mult mi-a fost dăruitor.

('The elm is my cousin and the oak is my brother, in good times and bad, they have always stood by me.' Quoted by Luiza Barcan in Ianus: Tradiţie şi Postmodernitate: Lemnul/Wood No 1, 2000.)

Sarmizegetusa is the name of an Iron Age citadel high in Romania's southern Carpathians. It was built by a people called the Dacians, whose empire once stretched from Transylvania to Moravia in what is now the Czech Republic. Sarmizegetusa was a royal fortress, the stronghold of King Decebal, the last Dacian leader whose territories had shrunk to the Transylvanian plateau. He was a force to be reckoned with. Decebal's men mounted raids south across the Danube into Roman territory and forced the Emperor Domitian to grant them concessions which were shaming to Roman pride. Dacia was of prime interest to the Romans because of its gold. Domitian's successor, Trajan, conquered Dacia in 106 AD. He kept the name for his new Roman province and replenished his coffers with gold from the Apuseni Mountains.

I have included Sarmizegetusa in the title of this book because of its symbolic place in the Romanian psyche.

It signifies to many Romanians what the city of St. David's does to the Welsh, St. Andrew's to the Scots or Camelot to the English. It was a real place with a thriving, self-sufficient community, a unique calendrical system and much else besides. However, much as it deserves a book to itself, it is Sarmizegetusa's symbolic meaning that made me want to use it. I could just as well have chosen to call the book 'Romania Destroyed' or 'Looking for Ecotopia'. If you are hoping to find a detailed description of Sarmizegetusa, and the Roman town to the north which was named after it, you will not find them here.

I started travelling in central and eastern Europe because the Berlin Wall came down at a time when I was sick of London. At the time I was an art journalist, and found what I was doing increasingly superfical. Czech friends who had fled Prague in 1948 had given me an appetite for a more reflective, less aggressively consumerist culture; it seemed possible to find it in places where 'progress' had been pulled to a rough full-stop. Romania came as a logical extension to journeys in the former Czechoslovakia and in Hungary.

15

The romantic image of Transylvania attracted me as it has so many Britons in the past.

My first experience of Romania left my head spinning: it was dreadful and wonderful – so much abject poverty going together with so much warmth and openness. I guess others have found the same thing in India, Mexico, Papua New Guinea and other places far from British shores, but to have it here, in Europe, seemed both bewildering and miraculous.

This book is therefore a pilgrimage, a fictional journey and a collection of true ones. Many of the people and all of the places are real (I have occasionally changed people's names to protect them). The official reason for putting these impressions down was that Romania is an extraordinary place, and few people who have not been there can appreciate its beauty and complexity. The unofficial one is that I needed Romania: while its craziness could be stressful - and hilarious - in the extreme, its sufferings were so much greater than mine that it offered a kind of healing. There was also the strength of its people's religious faith which, although certainly on the wane by comparison with what it had once been, was something that took me by surprise. It was mainly women who expressed their devotion to the church, and the church in question was mainly the Romanian Orthodox Church with its own Patriarch in Bucharest. There are other creeds in Romania, but Orthodoxy has the highest profile and, if you believe the official statistics, the largest number of members too. With hindsight I realise that the healing I found in Romania came from a few individuals whose faith and courage exceeded mine by miles. There were other reasons for going there, not least the sneering disbelief of a former acquaintance and Slavophile in London. When I told her where I was off to, she replied, "Romania! I wouldn't want to go *there.*" It had the reputation of a beaten dog, and the English countrywoman in me rose up in protective fury.

Between 1993 and the autumn of 2002 I went once, twice or three times a year, often alone, sometimes in company. From 1994 I was researching 'Blue Guide Romania'. I did my background reading in the British Library but it was somewhat drier than Bram Stoker's must have been. I wanted to avoid sensationalising a country that I barely knew; my aim was to give a fair and balanced view but not to pull any punches. The synthesis of what I found was this: Romania is a strange by-product of Marxism. While proclaiming that it represented the future, it had got stuck in the past. As I travelled around, it became clear that it was not only communism that held Romania back. By contrast with Britain, it had had no industrial revolution and no enclosures act, so in many areas the countryside looks unbelievably free of factory-made clutter. Although some places bear the scars of antiquated industrialisation, magnificent mountains enveloped in ancient, mixed forests cover a great part of the land and there are areas where you can walk for days and not see another human soul.

The more I came to know about Romania the more I questioned the terms used to describe its past and its culture: even the word 'backward' became irrelevant once I had been there long enough. It came to seem the height of rudeness to call Romania's small-holders subsistence farmers or peasants. Romanians have their own perfectly adequate word, 'ţărani', which means country people and covers the necessary eventualities without implying that they are simple-minded, poverty-stricken, second-class citizens.

The guide was published in 2000, but I still find the country deeply compelling. It has been described in so many ways, not always complimentary and occasionally downright rude. To me it is a bewildering, generous, funny, sometimes heart-breaking and frustrating, but never boring place that lies just far enough from western civilisation to make me think that western civilisation might not be all that it is cracked up to be.

Is Romania in eastern or central Europe, or in a new area called East-Central Europe? Romania is trying to reject its Balcanic image and stabilise its geo-political position in an increasingly polarised world. As a nation-state Romania is about the same age as Germany, but because it is emerging from a period of great isolation, sometimes it feels more like a brand new country struggling to unite historic and cultural differences. Hence the old adage that the Transylvanians are more hard-working and serious than the Wallachians who live across the Carpathians to the south and east. By the same token, middle-aged Wallachians often have an ingrained mistrust of Transylvanians, "those sneaky Ardeleni" as a friend in Bucharest once described them, who are in league with the Hungarians. As in the old Peter Cook and Dudley Moore sketch, both of them look down on the Moldavians. Yet it was in Iaşi, the Moldavian capital and home of Romania's first university, that an elderly Italian building contractor stopped me in the street to tell me that 'this is a land of miracles', assuming from the GB number plate on my car that I came from a less chaotic place. He was not being entirely ironic.

Writing can be a form of escapism. It lets you speculate freely about issues that are much harder to face in real life. Confronting the realities in present-day Romania takes a special kind of courage. Apart from being a travelogue, this narrative is also a tribute to the people who are doing that without losing their belief in the country, or in the fundamental differences between right and wrong. Last, but not least, it is also a gut reaction to a tragic circumstance: the loss of an ancient culture and ways of life that, while appearing poverty-stricken, could hold the key to an alternative life-style which is founded on principles that have a great deal to offer.

All over the world, these principles are being swept away in a tide of a corporate neo-imperialism. This tide influences what people want, what they buy, what they aspire to, how they think and live their lives. Big companies are interested in underdeveloped countries because they are full of potential new consumers of their products. This is not to say that improvements in health care, water supplies and sanitation, education, roads and communications should not be welcomed, when and if they arrive, but there is often a price for 'westernisation' that seems far too high. You only have to stand back a little from the hype surrounding it to see the damage which this process involves. It is easy to weep tears of nostalgia for something that has gone, or for something that is in the process of dying; it is much harder to save what is worth saving when few people agree on its value. It is also hard to tell beforehand whether a culture that is being threatened by a tidal wave will be able to get out of its way, or swim with the tide without being washed out. In Romania's case I do not have any easy answers to these questions. At the risk of clumsier metaphors, I hope that its people are clever enough not to throw their incalculable and invaluable riches away like the baby with the bath water.

On the walls of Suceviţa monastery in north-east Romania there is a row of paintings showing what happened to Adam and Eve after the Fall. It is called 'Adam's Contract with the Devil' and relates how Adam nearly sold his children's souls to Lucifer so that he could cultivate the land for food. It has some relevance today, and so the book is also a question. It asks if the philosophy behind this tidal wave of globalisation is as good for us as its pundits say. Lone voices in the wilderness have a habit of not being heard. In some places, though, they have become a chorus, and, odd as it may seem, Romania is one of them. My book ends with a 'case study'. I found out about the plan to open Europe's largest gold quarry at Roşia Montana in the Apuseni Mountains of western Transylvania while I was researching the guide book. Considering how valuable Roşia Montana is for its history and culture and its stunning land-scapes, to obliterate the place for dubious, short-term gain struck me as little short of a criminal act.

As I write this, in January 2003, people from Roşia Montana, Bucium, Corna and other affected villages are waging a campaign to save their homes and their mountains from being bulldozed to the ground. At the moment, the debate is being carried on between villagers who are pro and those who are anti, between the mining company and ecologists, between economists, bankers, investors, city slickers, all avid to make profits for their share-holders, and country folk who are far from simple but who feel vulnerable and betrayed. Questions about Roşia Montana's future are also being batted about between government officials and NGOs, between writers and archaeologists, idealists and pragmatists, romantics and realists. But the majority of people in the world has no idea that Roşia Montana even exists.

The question of whether or not this historic Romanian village should be turned into a quarry finally hit the Romanian newspapers in 2001; since then it has been discussed in the Romanian parliament and has been burning holes into dimly lit corners of cyberspace for months. There is a danger that the media hoo-ha could mask the basic issues but as yet, from this observer's point of view, all is not lost, and meanwhile some of those Romanians who felt powerless against any form of 'authority', no matter how flawed or illegal, may have gained confidence in the possibility of speaking out against injustice. Instead of the old response to every problem, 'Ce să-i faci?' (What's to be done?), usually spoken with a helpless shrug of the shoulders, there is hope in the very fact that they are standing up for their homes, their land, their environment, their futures and their heritage.

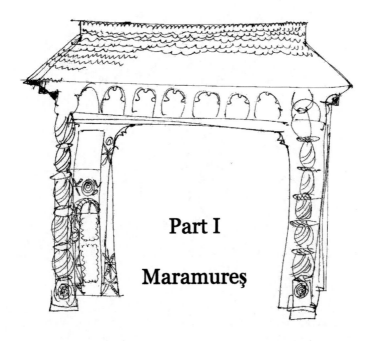

Part I

Maramureş

Viaţa omului şi viaţa lemnului sunt legate strâns. Ambele pleacă de la o sămânţa
şi se duc spre soare. Un copac care creşte singur ca şi un copil care creşte
singur, n-are viaţa frumoasă. Viaţa e cu atât mai frumoasă cu cât suntem mai
mulţi. Un lemn bătut de vânt are numai beteşuguri. E prins
de foc şi de secure.

('The lives of people and of wood are closely related. Both grow from a seed and
reach for the sun. A tree which grows alone is like a child that is
brought up on its own; it has a bad time. Life is much better when there are
many of us together. A tree that is battered by the wind
will always be sick. It is vulnerable to fire and the axe.'

From Luiza Barcan, op.cit.)

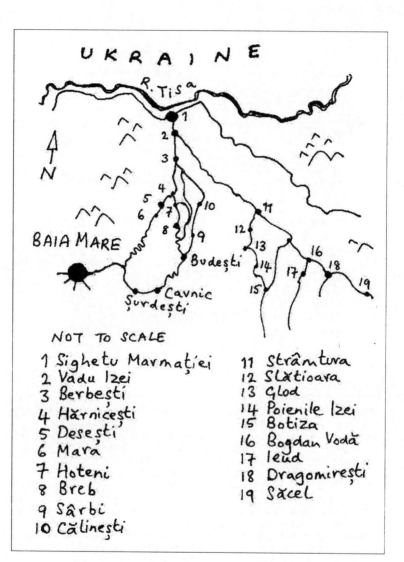

UKRAINE

R. Tisa

N

BAIA MARE

Budeşti

Cavnic

Şurdeşti

NOT TO SCALE

1 Sighetu Marmaţiei
2 Vadu Izei
3 Berbeşti
4 Hărniceşti
5 Deseşti
6 Mara
7 Hoteni
8 Breb
9 Sârbi
10 Călineşti

11 Strâmtura
12 Slătioara
13 Glod
14 Poienile Izei
15 Botiza
16 Bogdan Vodă
17 Ieud
18 Dragomireşti
19 Săcel

1

Behind the wooden curtain

It was nearing Christmas and I had been in Romania for four months. I was collecting material for a guidebook, but other issues kept getting in the way: it was more interesting to speculate on the history and beliefs of the country people than it was on the number of four-star hotels and the exact location of the train ticket office in such and such a city. But working on the guide had given me the chance to meet people in museums, cultural organisations and university departments, and I had a long list of contacts to draw on wherever I went. One place in particular had come up in conversations so often that its name was engraved in my brain.

Nowhere is the sense of deeply-embedded rural traditions more concentrated than in the north-western land called Maramureş. This is an isolated plateau of unbelievable beauty tucked away behind a barrage of mountains. Its isolation has given the Maramureş a special character. When the Romans conquered Dacia in 106 AD, they left inaccessible areas like this to their own devices. The Romans called the people who lived there 'free Dacians' and allowed them to stay independent. Soon a thriving trade developed between the communities on either side of the Roman lines. The free Dacians sold large quantities of gold, silver and salt to the Romans. What they got in return, apart from richer, was the knowledge of sophisticated Roman mining techniques. Nearly two thousand years later the communist government decided there was no point in collectivising this area. On the periphery, where they would not lower morale, the small farms carried on as before. Or if not exactly as before - Party authorities interfered in other ways - then with fewer disruptions, so that the land went on being cultivated and managed in the way that it had always been. You can see the difference: the farmers are more purposeful and less apathetic, and the countryside looks more cared for than elsewhere in Romania.

At the moment there is mining in Baia Mare, Cavnic and Borşa. So far, apart from the frightening exceptions of the cyanide spillages near Baia Mare and Borşa in 2000, rural Maramureş has been spared industrial devastation.

It did not always escape outside interference. In between the Romans who did not colonise and the communists who did not collectivise, the Hungarians and the Habsburgs dominated Maramureş. It was during occupation by the former that a landowner from the village of Cuhea in the Iza Valley gathered together a band of friends and kinsmen and decamped to the east across the Prislop Pass. Bogdan Vodă, as he was called, became the first independent prince of Moldavia. The year was 1359.

Maramureş was not completely cut-off from the outside world. Its present northern border is not a mountain range but the Tisa River, and across it lies the Ukraine. Until 1920, when Czechoslovakia received it, the land north of the river had belonged to Maramureş. Today only a third of the original territory of Maramureş remains. When the soviets took control the Maramureşeani who still inhabited the land north of the Tisa woke up to find themselves cut off from their relations in Romania. For forty years they could not see or speak to each other, and the handful of timber churches which had once been in Maramureş were all that was visible of their age-old Romanian connections. That is why the New Year celebrations in the border town of Sighetu Marmaţiei were so emotional at the end of 1989. For days and nights leading up to the annual festival, scores of people poured south across the river to be reunited with their long-lost families.

It is not entirely a myth that mountain people are hardier than the rest of us. The truth is that, in Romania at least, they have to be. Life in Maramureş is especially tough during the winter, and the incidence of arthritis and rheumatism among old and not so old is high. Life expectancy for Romanians as a whole is lower than the European average, and many of the people who live there would welcome an easier time. Large tracts of the country have no metalled roads, and in winter the dirt and stone roads become waterlogged and thick with mud. It is even more difficult to get around when the tracks are churned up by animals. In the 1980s tractors mysteriously disappeared, and most farmers were left with horses and oxen to do the heavy work. For the summer visitor, this state of affairs is one of the main factors that keeps the Maramureş looking so attractive. I feel about Maramureş as I do about a few personal belongings: I do not want anyone messing about with it.

But the question arises: what price should be put on this incredible charm if the people who live here cannot even move around?

The woodcarver of Breb

My first journey into Maramureş began one day in late autumn. I wanted to meet an old man who was known for making lovely wooden objects. His name was Petru Pop a Niţu and he lived in a village called Breb. On the day I arrived the weather was dry but the sky threatened snow. Driving with my partner Kit over the pass from Cavnic we lost our way. There were few road signs to guide us and our map did not cover this area in detail.

As we turned a corner we saw a woman making her way wearily along the road. She was short and stocky, with incredibly wide hips that made her full, knee-length skirt swing jauntily at every step. She was using a tall stick to help her get along, and she had a heavy-looking bag slung over her back. When we stopped to ask her for help, her healthy face with its direct blue eyes met ours in an off-putting scowl. After all, we were in a car and she was plodding along; we could hardly blame her for being less than enthusiastic about interrupting her journey. But as soon as she heard the name Breb, her expression changed. A seraphic smile lit her face, making her look twenty years younger, and she radiated warmth out of every pore. It was amazing  how hearing a name made this transformation. She put down her bag, straightened up with relief, and pointed back along the way we had come. Breb was the village where she had been born and raised. Now that the ice was broken, she wanted to know everything about us, why we were here, where we were from, where we were going. We did our best to explain and continued on our way, sorry that she was not coming with us.

A lot of rain had already fallen that day and we had to dodge the waterlogged potholes as we drove down the steep track into the village. Breb lay below us, a picture postcard village that has managed not to become a tourist trap. We soon found one of the reasons: the streets were a morass of mud. We parked the car and picked our way gingerly along the rough grass verges, looking for someone who could help us find Mr. Pop. On either side, the houses were made of wood and the households were separated by wooden palisade fences, some new, some weathered to a soft, grey colour. At the entrance to every one was a pair of tall timber gates. They were much higher than a man and in some cases reached 12 or 15 feet. The frame that supported them was constructed ingeniously to hold a side door and sometimes a seat as well, so that one side of the gateway was like a porch. Each gate had a narrow shingled roof which sheltered the whole ensemble. The vertical posts had raised patterns on them; some of them looked like ropes and had been curled into rudimentary stick figures or flower heads. Many of the gates were deeply weathered and leant heavily askew on their hinges; one or two were brand new and had been oiled to a bright orange colour. The gates were solidly functional, but also terrific pieces of sculpture.

We made for the old wooden church. For a large part of the rural population, especially the older ones, the church is more than a place to worship. It is a focal point for the community, a source of identity, culture and, usually, of warmth. In contemporary parlance, it provides 'social cohesion'.

Breb's wooden church had been made redundant and we were lucky to find anybody there at all. A group of men was practising ringing handbells in the churchyard next to the free-standing bell tower. Both church and bell tower were made of timber. The church roof was steeply pitched and at least three times higher than the walls, giving it a splendidly protected appearance rather like a hedgehog. But instead of spines it was covered with wood shingles, making the roof look as soft and velvety as sealskin.

The ringers were wearing thick, white homespun trousers and jackets bordered with black velvet. Each of them had on a 'clop', a straw hat shaped like an upturned flower pot and decorated with coloured ribbons and sequins. A two-litre bottle of plum brandy was being passed around among them.

As soon as I had explained who we were looking for, they swept us up in a wave of helpfulness. They escorted us to the school house, and we waited for a few minutes while one of the teachers fetched a little boy out of his class to take us to Mr. Pop's house. Breb primary school was a brick building of functional design; now the roof leaked and there was only the faintest suspicion of heating inside. The walls, painted an institutional green from the ground to shoulder height, looked cold. But the door opened on a class-room where twenty nine-year-olds were chanting the words of a Christmas carol, and the sense of coldness evaporated like breath on a frosty morning.

Our guide was called Călin. He led us back along the mucky street, and turned off into a path that wound zigzag fashion up through gardens, orchards, along narrow lanes and across the corners of fields. We traversed a stream by a bridge fashioned from a single tree trunk and climbed through gaps in hedges. At last, high above the village, we arrived at a farmstead where handsome, well-maintained timber buildings enclosed three sides of a sloping courtyard.

This was the home of Petru Pop a Niţu. It was a fascinating place. As well as sturdy barns for sheltering animals and storing machinery, in one corner of the yard there was a narrow, rectangular container with basket work walls. It was about ten feet high by six feet long and no more than two feet wide, and it was covered with a pitched and shingled roof. In Romania, farmers feed their livestock on maize cobs, and this prehistoric-looking container was designed to keep the cobs fresh through the winter. To me it was not simply a piece of equipment, it had personality. It was the same with so many other tools and structures that I saw in Maramureş: made by hand and based on models which had been passed on through many generations, they had acquired a simple authority that I found enormously pleasing. It was not only that they looked right for the job they had to do, but that they also had an element of fancifulness. This was something that I was sure the Romanian sculptor, Brâncuşi, had picked up on in his own work.

On the fourth side the property was open, so that we could look down uninterruptedly over copses and meadows to where a mist was rising from the village below.

The house was solid and chunky and hugged the ground. Its base was made of stone and contained a cellar. Above this were thick log walls which had been squared off, and a tall, pointed, shingled roof. There were steps up to the first floor living area which you reached by crossing an open verandah that ran along one side. The windows were small. They had been double-glazed in the traditional European way with a large gap between the inner and outer panes. Both inner and outer panes would open. The frames were painted light blue. Window and door frames were substantial pieces of wood, not skimpy apologies for bad design.

The plain wood of the beams, doors and door frames was dark with age. The house had two rooms separated by a narrow hallway. A large central beam stretched from end to end of the house, across the two living rooms and the hall. One of the living rooms was for guests. Three wooden beds stood next to the walls. They were covered in thick, shaggy 'cergi', the woven blankets with broad white and brown stripes which are popular in this area.

Petru lived here with his wife, his grown-up son and his son's wife and children. They were quietly-spoken, workaday people who made nothing of the fact that the old man was so skilled a craftsman. We sat on long wooden benches in the parlour-cum-kitchen and were asked to keep our voices low so as not to wake the baby, who was snoozing blissfully in a swinging wooden cot. An iron stove blazed in one corner, but there was no television, no telephone, no music centre, no radio. Embroidered cotton towels, made for decoration rather than for drying hands, hung festively from the walls. Some of them were draped around icons. Everything had a sense of rhythm, space and proportion that made you feel good to be there.

Petru Pop a Niţu is a grand name, and he uses it because it distinguishes him from all the other Petru Pops in the area. It bestows the image of a local celebrity, which in a quiet way he is. He is a slight figure and an old man now. His work is in demand far beyond the Breboaia and the Mara Valleys. Petru Pop a Niţu makes all kinds of things in wood, but his speciality lies in fashioning spindles with complex head pieces, decorated with finials and interlocking geometrical designs like the spires of fabulous churches, and

pocket-sized table crosses and wooden cups with ornamental handles for use in church services at Easter and Christmas. He makes the handles look like dragons' heads and cuts the wolf's-tooth pattern around the borders. The simple zigzag has been used by craftsmen in this area and in many others for thousands of years. Underneath each piece he inscribes the letters PACE, which means peace in Romanian. The spindles are used for pulling and twisting strands of wool into threads; the Romanian word for them is 'fus'.

Petru cut and shaped the wood by hand, and the wood he chose - cherry, apple, pearwood and spruce - came from the nearby orchards and forests. Because they were handmade his pieces were often rough and asymmetrical, but this quirkiness gave them an individuality that machine-made objects do not have.

We bought four wooden cups with zoomorphic handles like the snarling dragon-heads that the Dacians had used as a battle standard. Each handle had a zig-zag pattern around the rim and the bowls were no more than an inch or so across. Reluctantly we left the fire and made our way down the hill to Breb's main street. It was nearly dark. Kit offered Călin his silver pen-knife; the little boy took it politely and slipped away from us with a flashing smile that was half hidden by the dusk.

Real life in the Maramureş was not idyllic, but the old country ways were giving way to other systems that were not necessarily better. There was no denying that people here were suffering. Many had no running water in their houses, no internal plumbing, no telephone, they could sel-

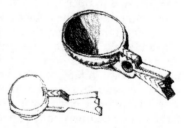

dom afford a car and more rarely a tractor; they cooked on wood-burning stoves with wood that they had to fell, season and cut themselves. But except for some of the poorest old people, they were not sorry for themselves; in fact their dignity was impressive. They treated us with simple, unaffected courtesy and expected the same in return. The experience was wonderful for a couple of escapees

28

from London, but it was confusing too. Whose reality were we inhabiting? It was hard to believe two such different places could exist in the same universe. One thing was certain: I had to come back to Maramureş.

Close encounters in Cluj

In the middle of the following summer I took a train from Braşov to Maramureş. It left in the late afternoon, a long blue worm trundling north-west across the Transylvanian plateau. I watched the sky darken from pale blue to ultramarine and a deep velvety purple. The light had an unearthly quietude, and like the atmosphere which lay over Romania itself, it was bewitching and bewildering by turns. It was pitch black by the time we arrived in Cluj, where I had to change onto another train to Baia Mare, the main town of Maramureş. Cluj, the capital of Transylvania, is a splendid Hungarian-Habsburg university city. It has towering apartment buildings decorated in voluptuous stucco, and hills and parks and tarnished memories. It used to pulsate with life and gaiety – or so I had read in Patrick Leigh Fermor's 'Between the Woods and the Water' – but now it too was shrouded in a silence that seemed uncanny for such an upstanding place, even if it was the middle of the night. I stayed in Cluj for twenty-four hours so that I could look around before moving on. My hostess was a sixty-year old archaeologist, the friend of a friend in London. Her name was Ioana and she lived with her widowed sister, Tora, and a grown-up nephew in one of those dilapidated flats that, with their layers of curlicued and patrician stucco, must have seen more gracious days. Ioana and Tora were educated gentlefolk who had survived the communist regime with their old, pre-communist values intact: they valued intelligence, honesty and plain-speaking, and they were staunch royalists. They laughed at their surroundings and pointed at the cracked walls and peeling wallpaper in their echoing flat, saying, "When we have money we will repair them". They were covering their sadness at the way things were now with a refusal to give into self-pity and a determination not to be defeated by their present circumstances. Although very relaxed, they had beautiful manners which reminded me of my music-loving grandmother's Viennese friends. Outside the old trams clanged and rattled past, making the walls shake. Even in Cluj, traffic noise has become a nuisance and the stink from the petrol and diesel fumes was nauseating after the fresh air of the mountains.

Ioana moved with the lively, eager grace of a red setter. She lived for a time when things would be 'right' again. In other words, this meant when the octogenarian King Michael would be restored to the throne. Apart from his age, the current political climate made it unlikely that Ioana's hopes would be fulfilled. They spoke their minds vigorously, without fear of listening ears or cowed servility. It was refreshing after my exposure to post-revolutionary Romania where I could feel the shadows of the suspicious past hovering over me even now, four years after the Ceauşescus were shot.

I had never met either of them before, but from the moment I walked through the door of their home Ioana and Tora treated me as though we had known each other for a long time. After a few brief courtesies, we found ourselves drawn together by a concern for the destruction of the natural environment and social values. This is as much of a threat in Romania as anywhere else. The drama of the Revolution was long gone, but the spirit which prompted so many to lay down their lives for freedom in December 1989 had not entirely vanished. In its disappointing afterglow, Ioana and Tora still carried a torch for what they believed the Revolution had been about: building a future in which people could develop their talents freely. It was so ironic when they found the wider world was not the place they hoped for; instead of a just and fair society where people cared for each other, what they had now was almost as bad as the one they had rejected, and in some cases worse. Instead of the caring, sharing community spirit they had fought for, everyone was out for him- or herself. From what the sisters could see, they were being actively encouraged to follow suit. But they would not. They had been educated differently and would defend their values to the end. I found myself thinking morosely that the 'culture' was against it, but maybe it was time for another revolution, global this time, which would put an end to the crazy waste which is contemporary capitalism. But who would listen to three middle-aged ladies commiserating over the state of the world in out of-the-way Transylvania? There was more chance of Dracula becoming a universally recognised symbol of peace.

If there was a surreal element to this family, it was not so much that they refused to give in, but that they maintained standards which had long since vanished from all but the most upper class households in Britain. They ate their meals from lovely porcelain plates, they drank tea by the pot-full - "Proper English tea," the sisters said, smiling at the misnomer and offering me a choice of Jacksons' tins from a trolley in the hallway, "Go on, have whichever one you want, you know best!" – and they ate in their lofty sitting room at a spindly inlaid table that had once adorned some magnificent breakfast room. The ghosts of Austro-Hungarian civility hung lightly in the air, and hovered over the clacking tiles of the parquet floors.

After they had busied themselves with all the necessary preparations for a civilised meal, we sat on chairs that were as elegant as they were uncomfortable. The table was lit by a graceful metal chandelier which had two working bulbs out of its potential seven. Meanwhile the nephew, who inhabited another time-frame in a parallel universe consisting of computers, nano-technology and cigarettes, kept away, hidden from sight behind a pair of enormous double doors. The family dog was there to, snuffling at us and whining to be let in. To my disappointment the sisters would not relent. I was not sure if this was because they feared he would knock me over, or the furniture, or both.

In the morning I had a chance to wander around the city on my own. Skirting the Roman excavations near the archaeology institute I was reminded of their grubby consequences. Breathing over the archaeologists' shoulders was the figure of the mayor, who wanted the digs to prove that the Romanians had a more powerful claim on Transylvania than the Hungarians. Crossing the little dog-eared square I found the statue of Romania's first eminent Roman historian, Daicoviciu. He looks appalled at the current state of affairs - he is covered in graffiti. I made a short-cut through an alleyway, and came across the rambling house where Matei Corvin (King Mattyás Corvinus of the Hungarians) was born. Then I came out into the busy street that contains the ethnographic museum, bookshops, a few cafés and other signs of university life.

Up and down this wide, straight road the houses have been washed in several shades of blue and yellow. The colourful façades help to defy the sense of gloom which threatens to descend on Romania's artistic and cultural life. So does the ebb and flow of students along the pavements. There is more to Cluj than pretty colours, and in term-time it is a lively place. It has two national theatres, one Hungarian, the other Romanian, an opera house, and several authoritative museums. They are housed in palatial buildings and stagger on in defiance of economic gravity, smelling of polish and scholarly reverence. Cluj has scores of churches too, proving once again that this is a multicultural city of broad interests. Manipulative politicians try to brainwash people into believing that one ethnic group has more rights than another, but its buildings, like its teachers and historians, tell a different story.

Later I tried to find out more about one of those teachers. I flagged down a taxi and went to the open air village museum. It was the first of its kind in Romania. Bucharest and Sibiu may have better collections, but the Cluj museum was the brainchild of a remarkable man. Romulus Vuia had the vision, shortly after Transylvania was united with the rest of Romania in 1918, to make a museum that would reflect all the ethnic groups living there. At the time, the

31

curators were spoilt for choice: traditional objects such as knee-high salt pestles made of wood, oil presses, dug-out canoes, New Year goat costumes and fulling mills were two a penny. Luckily they had the foresight to bring these pieces together and now we stare at them in wondering disbelief. I was the only visitor that afternoon; I had the feeling that most days were like that. It was like walking through a rural treasure trove: whole farmsteads, country inns and churches had been dismantled and reassembled on the hilltop. Decorated gateways and colourful pottery, glass icons and woven textiles, beehives scooped out of tree trunks: all had been placed in a virtual village setting, so that you could walk in and out of the houses and try to imagine what living in such conditions had actually been like. But fascinating as it was, the museum had an air of futility about it. Without people to bring the houses and objects to life, they looked empty and pointless.

It takes about three and a half hours to get from Cluj to Baia Mare by train. If you are lucky, Romanian train journeys are more than a means of getting from A to B. They can be social occasions, and depending on the circumstances the sociability can vary from pleasant encounters that leave you glowing with good humour to situations that make you wish you had emptied that bottle of water over somebody's head after all. In such a case, there are usually others around who feel just the same. There is nothing like shared outrage to break the ice. Given the state of most of the trains at that time, the best option was the Intercity which offered a reasonable level of comfort for three times the price of the normal express. In western European terms this amounted to a little extra outlay for a great deal of improvement.

Things have changed a lot since my first, exploratory train trips. Nowadays there are long distance coaches that provide an inexpensive, reliable and comfortable alternative to trains. On my second morning I caught a rattling express and filed into my seat with a group of countrymen and women for whom the Intercity could only be a dream. They looked as though they had been ground from the soil and would soon return to it; they had deeply-lined, deeply-sunburnt faces and eyes as sharp as buzzards'. Romanians are usually happy to talk, especially to foreigners. Although I could hardly speak the language I found out at first hand that signs and body language are effective substitutes, and if you are desperate you can always draw a picture.

The railway buffet does not exist except in Bucharest's main station, the Gara de Nord. There are no restaurant cars either, although you can buy cold, sweet coffee on the Intercity trains. Enterprising sweet-sellers tour the carriages during stops; they alternate with monks and deaf-mutes asking for alms. The sweets are usually bars of cheap, east-European chocolate; if you give money to the monks and deaf-mutes you get a little plastic coated picture of the Virgin Mary or a tiny gilded cross. Romanians prepare themselves for long train journeys by bringing their own sandwiches, drinks, a cushion and in winter maybe a blanket too: you never know when the heating may break down. They hate draughts. If you open a window you will provoke cries of protest, wagging fingers and a sharp "Nu e voie!" (That's not allowed!). When the ticket-collector came round, he said I was in the wrong compartment. Without a word, a young man got up, pulled my rucksack from the overhead net and gestured that I should walk ahead of him; thankful for his spontaneous help, I followed wordlessly.

Baia Mare: a pit on the edge of Paradise

I still wonder why, as we approached Baia Mare, I resented being accosted by a woman speaking to me in French. For some reason her attitude struck me as nosy. Perhaps that was the onset of a paranoia which is a hidden hazard in Romania. Foreigners are not immune. In any case I rejected her offers of help and chose to find my own way to the Hotel Carpaţi on foot.

I regretted my snootiness because it took me over an hour to reach the hotel and my rucksack weighed a ton. Dervla Murphy described the Hotel Carpaţi in her book 'Transylvania and Beyond'. It did not appear to have changed very much. I met the same uninterested attitudes – the receptionist stared right through me – and presumably the same stark décor. The room she consented to give me was coldly functional and had a huge black-and-white TV in one corner. It had a long row of buttons down one side but only one working channel; I could watch President Iliescu performing in the same eulogistic, fuzzy framework that must have graced his ill-fated predecessor. The day was mine and I spent the rest of it asleep. After all, as far as I knew, Baia Mare was nothing more than an industrial and mining town whose name means The Big Pit. All the guide books said so, and from what I could see it had little to recommend it beyond a railway station and a hotel.

Since getting to know it better, I have realised that Baia Mare has its saving graces. For one thing, it has another name. When the Hungarians captured it, sometime back in the 1500s, they were persuaded not to raze the citadel to the ground by the timely intervention of a group of girls. Their pleas worked better than the terrified citizens could have hoped. The walls stayed up, and sections of the medieval fortress are there to this day. For a long time afterwards Baia Mare was known as 'The Town of the Young Ladies'. If it is only a matter of one ancient square and a few hectares of ramshackle terrace houses which radiate around it, then the town has a history, and that history gives it identity and pride. But it takes a practised eye to recognise the beauty under the hangdog look and the grim, regimented blocks that have grown up around it. Look carefully and you will see stone walls which are more than three yards thick. There are houses of handsome proportions from the Hungarian and Habsburg periods, but no one seems interested in rescuing them. To me they stand out as evidence of a past that was not always crippled by a disastrous economy nor poisoned by sulphurous fumes.

When I went downstairs to eat, the hotel lobby was full of men in leather jackets. I pushed through the glass doors into the unfriendly restaurant. Supper was a solitary affair during which I toyed with a 'friptura' of fried veal, boiled potatoes and raw white cabbage soaked in vinegar. There was a different receptionist behind the desk and I asked her for a phone line to a woman in Deseşti, the village I had arranged to visit on the following day. The connection had to be made through the village exchange, an antediluvian system that demanded fluency, determination and a very loud voice. The number I had been given had only two digits.

A Rattling Good Ride

I have a great affection for buses because they are social levellers. In the 1960s the bus I caught to school carried the eye-catching advertisement: Go with Worth's for a Rattling Good Ride. The bus to Deseşti looked a lot more antedeluvian than my school bus. It could have been built in the 1930s and was old, curvaceous and creaky. Knowing I had to get in or get stuck, I decided that it had personality. It had floral curtains that were drawn tight over the windows, as though the passengers could not bear to look out. The springy brown plastic seats were far too short for my legs. The map showed that the distance between Baia Mare and Deseşti is only a matter of 40 kms or so; the journey was scheduled to take three hours.

"Curentul, curentul! Închideţi fereastra!" The dratted draught again. There was no way that the woman behind me would tolerate the mild zephyr which I had inflicted on her by yanking the window open. She gestured vigorously that I should shut it again immediately. The bus barely managed thirty miles an hour. Its gears made desperate, ear-splitting noises and the body rocked from side to side, more like a boat in a storm than a four-wheeled vehicle on a quiet country road. However if the drive was long it was also a revelation. We seemed to be travelling back through time. The road from Baia Mare to Desești climbs up the Guțâi Pass, zig-zagging upwards through the dense forest in a series of ear-popping bends. About half-way up you come to the simple monument that marks the grave of Pintea Viteazul, a Robin Hood figure who fought against the Habsburgs for a free Maramureș. Someone pointed it out for me, but there was hardly anything to see. The stone plinth is more useful as a marker for gauging where you are.

At the top of the pass there was a café. It was not much more than a layby with a shack attached: somewhere to get out, stretch your legs and have a smoke. There were one or two white plastic tables and inside the dark hole of the café everyone had congregated to buy tiny cups of cold sweet Ness, the powdered Nescafé that comes in huge tins. It was sold as a substitute for Turkish coffee, but there was no way of heating water. I guessed that this was a state-owned enterprise and the proprietors were rationing electricity. In such surroundings minor inconveniences such as this did not matter. Around us were tall beech and fir trees that filtered the sunlight and smelt of freedom. Faded signs warned people not to set fire to the woods. Someone said that the forests had been preserved so that Ceaușescu could come and hunt here. The air was clean and fresh, and the puffs of wind that swept over us were a summons to start living. I stuffed my sweet-papers into my pocket and climbed enthusiastically on board.

Compared with the tortuous ride we had just endured, the journey down the northern side of the Guțâi Pass was a breeze. We nose-dived into the hairpin bends. Every so often there was a break in the forest cover, giving glimpses of other mountain ranges that flew away as far as the eye could see. Human beings have managed the land for thousands of years, yet there was no evidence of the intense monoculture which impoverishes so many parts of western Europe. If Ceaușescu had been responsible for the mind-expanding landscape that was unfolding before me, he might have deserved some praise. But his primary interest was in shooting the Carpathian bears, not in sustaining the ecology.

It seemed a long time before there was any sign of human habitation. Eventually we began to pass discreet timber houses that stood like brave pioneers at odd intervals, overshadowed by tall, dark spruce trees, a few yards back from the road side.

Through the looking glass: The Mara Valley

Suddenly we were in Mara. The village takes its name from the river that flows through it. The stream is shallow, sometimes little more than a trickle from the springs that rise in the surrounding mountains. On its way north it gathers strength from other brooks, and merges with other rivers until it reaches the Tisa, which separates Romania from the Ukraine. The main road to Sighetu Marmaţiei slices through the village. On either side are houses with small, neat front gardens, or timber farmsteads. Usually the houses were planted gable end to the road as in rural Hungary and Slovakia. The Empress Maria Theresia had introduced the system, and it was a mark of Austrian practicality. Responsible for the deaths by burning of I cannot guess how many Orthodox priests, she had made the roads wider too, to reduce the risk of spreading fire.

From the bus, I could see houses with solid wooden walls the colour of molasses. They had wide window frames painted green or blue. The fences were made of wood, and here too there were tall timber gateways like the ones I had seen in Breb. Here and there a proud housewife had hung her enamel cooking pots on the branches of a dead tree. Red, green, brown and white, spotted and plain, battered and new, they looked like Christmas decorations and were clearly meant to impress.

The road is the main artery, and pathways and stony lanes join it like blood vessels. The road brings everyone together, but forces them apart as well. Perhaps I was oversensitised by the vulnerability of this magical landscape: after all, a road is just a road. But it seemed to me like a knife that was cutting through the flesh of Mara's rural tranquillity.

Sturdy, four-square, broad-hipped women in floral scarves, white blouses and black skirts swung along the roadside. Some waved cheerily at the bus driver, others concentrated on their own business. The sexes seemed to keep apart. Men stood around talking to each other; they wore battered felt hats, open-necked shirts, grey trousers tucked into black gumboots: the same farmers' uniform that can be found in California and New South Wales. A buffalo brushed herself vigorously back and forth against a hedge, using it as a back scratcher. She made a contented grunting noise as she moved, and her long, aristocratic snout disappeared into the foliage. As she moved slowly forwards, the buffalo left a trail of leaves and twigs. Nobody appeared to mind; this was rural Romania, not Surrey, after all. Other forms of transport materialised out of nowhere. They evoked a world I had thought long since dead. There were horses and oxen pulling long, narrow, V-shaped wooden carts, sturdy sit-up-and-beg bicycles, and the old-fashioned Renault 12 cars that Romanians call Dacias. The Dacia is perfectly suited to Romaania's roads and prevailing economic conditions: it is as bouncy as a Chesterfield sofa and repairs cost next to nothing. It is both Romania's Deux Chevaux and its wannabe Porsche. I have seen one with its back seat so full of apples that its rear end banged along the ground. I have seen Dacias on their way to market with a boot full of piglets, and souped-up versions with spoilers and flames along their sides. But in Mara the Dacias were mostly white and riddled with rust.

Mara used to be called Crecești. I picked this up in the inconsequential way you do when researching guidebooks but I never discovered why its name had been changed. At the southern end of the village, next to the tarmac road, there was a cartway and gate built into the same framework. It was the same basic type as the ones I had seen in Breb and Cluj, but this one was simpler and more beautiful. It was also much smaller. The wood was so old and ramshackle that it could easily have been mistaken for a piece of workaday carpentry thrown together just to make do.

Instead of close-fitting vertical slats which prevented you from seeing inside, the cartway gate was made of six horizontal struts braced by a vertical piece. What made it unusual was its roof and the doorway to the right hand side of the cart entrance. The shingled roof provided generous cover from sun and rain on all sides. The door was made in a herringbone pattern. It was set into the framework of the gate, and above it was a circular opening. This was decorated with four spokes radiating from a central medallion. The motifs included ropework figures and solar symbols, and something that looked very like a tree of life.

The vertical struts which held the roof up on either side were jointed and splayed at the top, making a curved frame around the opening. It was just enough to make the structure look less than ordinary, but not fussy. Sturdy and dignified but not austere, the gate seemed to sum up the character not only of the architecture of Maramureş but of its people as well.

"Cine sunteţi?" The man leaning over a neighbouring gate aimed the question at me like a tennis serve.

"Sunt o englezoaica; sunt in vizita."

"Anglie? Oh, departe, departe. Vă place România?" How could I explain how much I liked but could not understand Romania, that in far-off England we did things so differently, but not necessarily any better?

Exits and Entrances

The ramshackle gate in Mara was a shadow of its former self. Its narrow roof tree was starting to cave in and many shingles were missing, but on the ridge there was a row of silhouettes in the shape of picks and axes. They were meant to invoke good spirits who would look after the household and frighten witches away. It was part of the symbiosis between religious and pagan beliefs that made rural life here so potently mysterious. The Mara gate had been bought by the local ethnographic museum, but the owners still wanted it and so the museum let it stand in the place for which it had been made.

The carpenter had inscribed a date on the gate post. It said 1938 - more recent than I had supposed. Two horses trotted past pulling a cart. They had bright red tassles on either side of their browbands. Not so long ago the tassles had been used to protect the animals from the evil eye; now they were more of a fashion statement.

Eventually the owners of Mara's oldest gate got tired of having an irreparable antique at their front entrance. It has been dismantled and sent for safe-keeping to the village museum in Baia Mare.

An ethnography lesson

Studying the Mara gate reminded me of the ethnography lessons I had received in Bucharest. My teacher there had been Alina, a woman in her early fifties who was finishing a PhD on kinship. Alina was a phenomenon in her own right. She pursued her subject with a fearsome passion and a single-minded dedication. She was like a handful of Romanian scholars whom I had already met. These were people who clung to their belief in their work even though the world at large had become indifferent to its value. Alina was a strange mixture of old-fashioned correctness and modern sophistication; she had attended conferences in the USA and had studied at Berkeley, but she had grown up in a privileged environment and somehow retained its standards during the alien regime. Her life had continued quietly in one of those curious backwaters in the centre of Bucharest that had survived relatively unblemished by Ceauşescu's depradations.

We first met in Mihai Pop's house. In his late eighties, Mihai Pop was the grand old man of Romanian ethnography. He knew everyone who was worth knowing in the field, and Alina had been his student. With her rasping laugh and acute perceptions, she was a daunting figure. I was thrilled but apprehensive when she agreed to help me learn more about Romania's traditional ways of life.

Alina invited me to her institute. A tall and stately Neo-Classical building from the days of the city's lazy opulence, it was hidden away from passers-by behind a high wall and a wrought-iron gate, thirty seconds walk from Bulevardul Magheru, one of Bucharest's main shopping streets. I crossed a handkerchief-sized courtyard planted with box hedges and climbed dark stairs to a spartan classroom with high windows. Alina lectured me about Romania's archaic social structures: scattered, nucleic and ribbon settlements, and the predominance of 'free' villages over feudal ones. She spoke good English, but assumed a level of knowledge I did not have. Realising this, she would stop every so often to see if I had understood.

"The villages in the Maramureş were traditionally free. In mountain areas like that, in Vrancea in southern Moldavia, and especially in the Apuseni where the Moţi people have lived for thousands of years, you get scattered villages that look completely haphazard. They are the oldest surviving settlements in this country."

Alina impressed on me that Romanian folk art was different from other varieties because it had been created without a fear of empty spaces. Her words about restraint in decoration came back to me as I got to know the Maramureş and could verify what she said. There was less busy-ness in the older carvings than in the newer ones, at any rate. Her remarks also seemed pertinent when I had a chance to look at the 18th century palaces and monasteries built for Constantin Brâncoveanu, the Golden Prince of Wallachia. His artists developed a Romanian version of the Baroque style that was particularly cool.

I remained in awe of Alina until she started asking how she would be received in English society. She had only been to London for a few days, and was anxious for my opinion.

"Tell me, if you don't mind the question, but I have to ask you. What would English people think of my clothes? How would they react to my voice, my accent, my manners? Would they think I was very common and vulgar?" We were having a bite to eat in Bucharest's brand new Pizza Hut, where the concept of fast food was being introduced to a city more at home with long, lingering lunches and Mediterranean time-scales. I started to laugh, not out of malice but from disbelief at the thousand-mile gap between my country's class system and hers. It was impossible to say which was the most outdated.

Alina knew Romania like the back of her hand. She loved her country and was proud of its deeply-rooted culture. She shared her knowledge without reticence, never bullying me but impatient that I should get the right message. Once she had decided to like me, she asked me round to see her flat. She lived in a pleasant concrete and glass building dating from the 1960s. It stood in a lane of two-storey villas, some of which had been built in the 18th century. The lane was asphalted but the tar had cracked in many places, letting the original cobbles show through. In an adjacent street were the crumbling remains of a 'han' or caravanserai. Its courtyard was large enough to accommodate strings of pack horses, and I tried to imagine the travellers who might have leant over the balconies to supervise their merchandise being unloaded for safekeeping. Nearby lived a former Czech Olympic athlete who was restoring a row of medieval cottages. They were tucked away behind a nondescript wall - you would never guess they were there. A village atmosphere pervaded several parts of Bucharest: cocks crowed in the mornings and, until the city fathers banned them in 1995, pigs lived next to grand town houses, adding a distinctive rural flavour to the petrol scented air.

A giant Paulovna tree draped its branches over most of Alina's front garden, and she could touch its leaves from her fourth floor balcony. Her flat had one largeish room which functioned as bedroom, study, sitting and dining room. The kitchen and bathroom were no bigger than cupboards and you could barely stretch your arms out in the hall. The walls were lined with books, and papers covered most of the other available surfaces. On the floor Alina had placed a beautiful Oltenian rug with a motif of flowers enveloping the figure of a dancing woman. There was just enough room for Alina's enthusiastic and hairy dog. Alina loved animals and her field work had made her sensitive to wildlife in the city. In a corner of her balcony wall a dove was sitting on a nest of eggs. If you listened very carefully, you could hear her mewing softly. From the balcony you could see a roofscape of Parisian mansards, pale buff-coloured stone and grey slate and Byzantine domes. For a moment you could imagine that the dislocation that Ceauşescu forced on his capital had never happened.

"You know," said Alina, serving homemade apple strudel on porcelain plates, "I really love my work. I am totally dedicated, so much so that I once spent a night in a hay barn. There was nowhere else to sleep, and when I got up the next morning, I counted twenty-eight ticks attached to my body!"

2

Eight days in Deseşti

Deseşti is the next village after Mara as you travel north. The bus pulled in to let me off, and the other passengers watched curiously as I dragged my rucksack from the seat in front and shuffled it down the steps. Outside, five short, stocky, broad-hipped women wearing knee-length skirts, cardigans, and head-scarves like the woman from Breb were chatting to each other in a circle. They turned to look at me in my jeans and short hair. Their stares were not rude, just interested and a bit cautious. We stood within feet of each other, looking across a cultural gulf that was decades wide. I had come full of confidence that my world was more up to date than theirs, but now I'd got here, none of them was the odd one out: I was.

The woman I was going to stay with had asked me to ring her from the exchange. It was not difficult to find. While most of the village is hidden from the main road, the 'civic centre' is compact and lies less than a catapult's shot from the bus-stop. It comprises the village school, a couple of wood cabins which operate as shops or bars, the village hall, the police station and the phone exchange. Most of these buildings were flat-roofed, and made of breeze block which might or might not have been faced with concrete; if Ceauşescu had had his way the entire village would have looked like them. But his programme of bulldozing the old settlements and raising modern 'agricultural centres' with high-rise flats in their stead got little further than the outskirts of Bucharest. As sociologists later discovered, the old people who had given up their small farms and animals to move into these cold and echoing blocks died within six months. Although some modern brick villas with hacienda-style balconies and zinc roofs were going up, most of the houses in Deseşti were made of timber with steeply pitched roofs covered in shingles.

I pushed through the creaky glass door into the exchange. A glass partition separated the operator from the public, and there were two chairs and a table for people waiting in the narrow hallway. Hanging around for a line could take ages. The operator pulled open a small hatch and smiled enquiringly at me. I handed her a piece of paper with my hostess's number on it. She pulled some plugs out of the console in front of her and pushed others in, deftly switching from one line to another as though she were playing a complicated musical instrument. She dialled a number on a black bakelite phone. I could hear the bell ringing at the other end of the line, then there was a click, a crackle and a disembodied voice yelled "Da?" into the void. A brief conversation ensued, then the operator smiled at me again, put the handset back in its cradle, and made signs that I should sit down.

"Cinci minute," she said, and turned back to her work.

Five minutes later Parasca came to meet me. She was named after Paraschiva, one of Romania's most popular Orthodox saints, but I soon learnt that most people called her Paşa. She was a handsome, dark-haired woman in her early forties, taller than average for her country, and she had a fruity, husky laugh, the result of smoking, drinking and hiding her loathing of communism as best she could. Paşa had recently married a journalist from Baia Mare. Her husband was younger than she was and they had no children. Just after the Revolution Paşa's husband had helped to found a royalist newspaper called *Expres*; it had not survived long, and in his frustration and disappointment he had turned to drink. He spent most of his time in town, where the couple had a small flat; Paşa had a teaching job in Baia Mare, but during the holidays she stayed in Deseşti to look after her widowed mother.

Luckily for me, she was fluent in French. We struck up a stilted conversation while we walked up the stony lane between rows of farmsteads with magnificent gates and fenced-in gardens, patterned neatly with cosmos and chrysanthemums in alternating rows with cabbages, onions and beans. The farmhouses were clustered together in the village as they were in Breb, and as they had once done in England before the 17th century enclosures. Dogs barked. Cockerels crowed. Cattle and oxen lowed. There were no cars. God seemed to be in his Heaven.

A chuckle of bantams scuttled out of the way as we entered their farmyard, their necks working jerkily as they scattered in panic to the four winds. Paşa's mother, who was now in her seventies, owned a small-holding, and in the attractive timber barn opposite the house she kept a solitary cow. There was a stand-pipe to one side of the yard; she used it to do her washing. Beyond the yard was a small orchard of plums, apples and apricots. A pathway led through it to the house next door which belonged to Paşa's brother. The trees and blackcurrant bushes were loaded with fruit. We were only a quarter of a mile from the dusty high road, but there was an atmosphere of plenitude: everything seemed to be flowering or bearing fruit, taking its time without harrassment. There was an occasional rumble of a cart going up or down the lane.

"Tu es fatiguée? Eh bien, viens dans la maison. Tu peux reposer une heure ou deux et puis nous mangeons ensemble." Paşa's

French was easier for me to understand than the Parisians'. She was right, I was dog tired after my rattling good ride but, like a child, almost too excited to sleep.

Paşa showed me into the house. It was the traditional kind, with thick log walls. We climbed a short stairway to the living quarters. They were divided into the part the family used all the time and the 'guest' rooms that Paşa and her mother left untouched except for special occasions. It was odd when they had so little space to work with anyway, but it made heating the house easier. We walked into the kitchen, which was minute and had a small wood-burning cooker, a single electric bulb with no shade, a dresser for storing crockery and cooking pots, and a large bed which belonged to Paşa's mother. She had a rocking chair on the balcony, but there were no upholstered seats. Through a door in the back of the kitchen was another bedroom. The bed was covered with striped 'cergi' and on the floor there was a striking flat-weave carpet decorated with geometrical designs. I slept more soundly than I had for weeks.

Over the next eight days, Paşa became my guide, supplying me with details of local history, ethnography and wildlife. Her father had been the village priest, and as a result she had been educated to university level. It gave her a status which opened most doors in the village. As we strolled through Deseşti one morning I asked her about the ornamented gates.

"They used to be a badge of the Nemeşi - the local Romanian nobility," she told me. The gates are still a sign of prestige but the concept of a local aristocracy is vanishing. The newest gates had bulbous pillars that looked like crude imitations of Brâncuşi's Endless Column and they were decorated like harvest loaves, varnished to a bright orange and hung with great wooden chains. They would have been perfect at the entrance to a MacDonald's. But the older ones were beautiful; their patterns were more discreet and less fussy. Again there was the striking rope pattern which ran vertically up the pillars, twisting here and there into crosses or coiled into stick figures or rosettes. There were other circular patterns enclosing sunburst motifs or crosses.

"The figures that look as though they are made of rope are very old indeed; I mean we can see them in Bronze Age designs found in this area! And you know that these round patterns are sun motifs that come from the Persians. But designs like these have been found in Thracian ornamentation too," she added, deepening the sea of influences and cross-currents, images and thoughts that was sloshing about in my head.

"Is there a special type of wood culture here?" I asked rather idiotically. She did not put me down.

"For sure," she said, "because there has always been so much wood in this region. There's something else besides: wood is a more human and intimate material than stone. Unfortunately" - she waxed more lyrical - "it is more fragile, like our lives, and so the traces of this culture have disappeared. But I believe that the memory of this special relationship with the forests lives on; it is reborn every time someone makes a wooden tool or builds a timber house."

The forests had been managed since man arrived, but for once the management had been tactful. The trees grew naturally, not dragooned into the tight formations of a deathly monoculture but cascading over the mountain sides and pastures in a variety of species, giving shape, shelter, dignity and meaning to the landscape. In the far distance, twenty miles away, the forests gave way to mountains that rose to a crest like a cock's comb. That was its name: Creasta Cocoşului. The peaks were now being promoted as a tourist resort, but Dacian miners had dug for gold and silver on the topmost ridge. The mining industry was still nibbling at the edges of Maramureş. I wondered how invasive it would become.

"Pe cine căutaţi?"

Who was I looking for? The old woman asked me this as I dawdled on the path leading up from Paşa's house. I was not looking for anyone, but soaking up the extraordinary scenes that unfolded before me like a child's picture book.

Bordering the village, wild woodland linked fingers with the open meadows, the orchards and rectangular stands of maize and corn. Fences were there to keep animals out rather than in; nothing was parcelled off, nothing gave the impression that trespassers would be prosecuted. It was an amazingly liberating sensation. And the prettiness had not been landscaped as though for a single, wealthy landowner; it was shared and had a purpose. I felt at one with the world.

A history lesson

The central Asian people known as Magyars or Hungarians began exploring the land that became Romania in the 9th century. They had already migrated west from the Don and were settled in the plains of Pannonia (The Great Hungarian Plain) but Transylvania attracted them because of its great forests, and the promise of mineral wealth in the mountains and the fertile plateau beyond. Their name for this territory was 'Erdély', the forest land, just as in Latin it was known as Transylvania, the land beyond the forest. The Hungarians did not conquer all of the Transylvanian plateau at once, but moved east in stages. The first documented Magyar district in the

Maramureş dates from the beginning of the 14th century. In other areas the Hungarians sent the Székély people to guard the regions that they had newly conquered. Called Szeklers in English, they were a mysterious race whose origins are unclear: some experts say they were Germanic, while others maintain that the Szeklers were Turkic and followed the Magyars in their westward migrations. The Szeklers had settled in eastern Transylvania and preserved many old customs including that of writing in runes. I had never heard of the Szeklers having been in Maramureş and wondered if their culture had filtered north into this isolated plateau.

The Hungarians converted to Christianity in 1000 AD and joined the Roman Catholic Church. A clash between the two branches of Christianity divided the Orthodox east from the Catholic west in 1048, and the invading Catholics did not tolerate the Orthodox Church in Transylvania. The first Hungarian king to focus his attention on the Maramureş was the Angevin Károly I Róbert. Many Maramureşean nobles bitterly resented his interference and some rose up against him. Under the Angevins, preference was given to those who adopted Catholicism and took Hungarian names, although the Catholics were happy to accept the aid of 'schismatics' when it came to fighting the Turks in Dalmatia and the Balkan peninsular. The Catholics' intolerance of Orthodoxy was the trigger that made some of the Maramureş lords establish their own, Orthodox principality in Moldavia in around 1359. Pockets of Orthodoxy survived in the area, but when the Habsburgs occupied Transylvania in the late 17th century, they offered what they believed to be an ingenious solution to the conflict. It was called Greco-Catholicism, or the Uniate Church, and it allowed followers of Orthodoxy to retain their rites in return for some face-saving changes. What the Habsburgs saw as being good for Transylvania was equally appropriate for the Maramureş.

Greco-Catholics: a subtle compromise

Greco-Catholicism was invented at the Council of Florence in the 15th century. Western leaders needed Balkan soldiers to help them withstand the Turkish advance, and had to find a way of putting their differences aside. The idea was to introduce four main changes to the Orthodox rite. Orthodox believers found two of them hard to swallow: one was that the Pope should replace the Patriarch as the Church's human leader, and the other introduced something called 'the *filioque* clause' to the Creed. *Filioque* means 'and the Son', and it signified that worshippers would have to place Jesus incarnate on the same spiritual level as God the Father and the Holy Spirit: three-in-one instead of two.

The ideological debate about the nature of Christ - whether he was human or divine - had been thrashed out in some of the earliest Christian councils, and Orthodox churchmen took the issue very seriously. Pragmatism won the day. The most influential Orthodox monastery in Maramureş was the Exarchate of Peri. It had been founded in the 14th century and had the right to train its own monks. Peri lay to the north of the River Tisa, and in the anti-Habsburg uprising of 1703-11 it was completely destroyed. With it vanished the greatest opposition to the Uniate Church. At the eastern end of Maramureş was the monastery of Moisei, famous today for organising an annual Akathist parade in honour of the Virgin Mary. The abbot was in close touch with his opposite numbers in northern Moldavia, and his disgust with the whole idea was practically palpable. By and large, the people of Maramureş accepted the change, and thereafter the country became predominantly Greco-Catholic.

The little church on the hill

So did Deseşti's oldest church. Paşa's father the priest was now dead, and his place had been taken by a younger man who kept a small-holding as well as looking after his human flock. We walked up the hill from Paşa's house to see her father's grave. The church stands on the top of a hill surrounded by a cemetery and scattered prunus trees. The cemetery was full of tombs bedecked with colourful flowers. Between them the grass grew long, and haughty cockerels with glossy plumages roosted on the graves without a by-your-leave. Some of the graves were marked with plain wooden crosses that had sunk into the ground. Others were made of black-painted metal wrought into decorative arabesques. The crosses had semicircular hoods and the names of the dead were painted on the stems in white lettering done by hand. Someone had tied long, blue ribbons on them, and these were fluttering in the wind as though for a party whose guests were temporarily missing. Beyond the official cemetery among the apple trees was a group of unmarked grassy mounds; this was unhallowed ground where suicides had been buried.

The present building is relatively new - it dates from 1770. Its layout is modelled on the Byzantine basilica, but its outline is Gothic. From a door at the west end you walk into an outer chamber or *pronaos* with a low, flat ceiling, where women once worshipped separately from the men. A wooden partition stands between it and the *naos*. This is the largest room in the church, and its ceiling rises to a barrel vault which lies directly underneath the pointed roof.

The screen is organised in horizontal rows, with Christ at the top, and the most important saints below him. At the bottom of the screen are larger icons of the patron saint, Christ, and the Blessed Virgin. The icon screen protected the altar from the eyes of everyone but the priest, except during services when the Imperial Doors were thrown open to reveal the cross and the embroideries bathed in radiant candlelight. Deseşti's wooden church is a gem of a building; from a distance it looks as though you could hold it in the palm of your hand. It is dedicated, like Paşa, to the globe-trotting Saint Paraschiva whose relics were brought from Constantinople to Moldavia in 1641.

Like many of its 90 or so fellows which survive in this part of Romania, Deseşti's church benefited from skills which had been honed to perfection over hundreds of years. The Gothic influence came from southern Transylvania, where Saxon colonists built burly citadel churches in stone. But these churches were something else. What was rugged in Transylvanian Gothic became light and elegant in these timber ones.

It is their steeply-pitched, softly curved and shingled roofs that give them their special character. In Maramureş a second layer continues the shape of the upper one. In Deseşti the tower is square and has a lookout platform at the top; above this the tower comes to a point with a smaller turret on each of its four sides. The turrets were borrowed from the Gothic of the Transylvanian Saxons too. They used to show that the village had the right to enact its own laws. Deseşti church is chunky and solid, but its lines, sweeping upwards to the sharp ridge and the point of the spire, give it great dignity. On the outside, the decoration is sparing: a raised ropework belt encircles the body of the church and frames the door at the west end. The squared-off logs which form the walls and brace the great weight of the roof are held together with interlocking joints. There is a long bench on one side of the building where the roof hangs wider and lower than the other; on special days the old folk come to sit here and receive gifts of food and alcohol.

Paşa suggested that we should go to the church during a women's service. Never one for religious rites, I accepted through curiosity rather than piety. They were mainly old ladies and little girls: most of the inbetweeners were out at work. The old women sat on benches flush with the walls; one of them beckoned me over to sit beside her. An unaccompanied choir sang in the naos. The choristers, who were dressed in their own clothes, stood facing the icon screen, which was decorated with embroidered towels. A hanging candelabra provided an intimate, flickering light, and small candles had been placed on the floor near favorite icons. When the Imperial Doors were thrown open, we were momentarily dazzled by the blaze from the altar.

Having been reluctant to stay long, I found myself wanting to sit there for hours. The paintings that covered the walls and ceilings could hardly be seen because they were covered in black waxy grime and mould. Since then they have undergone a marvellous transformation, thanks to UNESCO and a team of restorers from Bucharest who have cleaned the frescoes, revealing a positive wonderland of Neo-Byzantine folk art under the soot and grime. Its centrepiece is a superb tree of life set in a paradise garden, showing the intimate symbiosis between Christian stories and archaic folklore. In this setting the relationship seemed particularly vivid.

The painter had been a local man. His nam was Radu Munteanu. He outlined his figures in thick black lines, and coloured them with a mixture of vegetable and mineral pigments. He laid the colours on a thin layer of gypsum which had been plastered straight onto the log walls. The gaps in the logs were covered by strips of canvas glued on with size. Radu was inspired by the frescoes on the great medieval churches in Moldavia, where the Last Judgment, the Jesse Tree, the Prayer of All Saints and other classic themes from Orthodox iconography can be seen both inside and out.

"Îți a plăcut serbătoarea?"

Yes, I had liked the service. The words of the hymns and the liturgy had passed over my head in a pleasant if incomprehensible stream. I was glad I had not had to stand all the time.

From the hill beside the church you can see right across the wide valley floor. On the horizon is the jagged-edged Cock's Comb, the highest peak in the Guțâi range.

Customs and Cosmetics

When she had time to relax I asked Pașa to tell me about free villages in the Maramureș. It was lucky that she loved to talk.

"There is one not far from here called Mănăstirea." The name means monastery, but the monks of Mănăstirea have long since gone. "We had free villages here because the Maramureș is so isolated; people built houses in the forests and helped themselves to the timber. Gradually communities developed; they organised their own system of rules and had their own councils and leaders. It was long before the Hungarians came," she added, helping to orientate me. "Every farm knew how much land it had and nobody bothered with formal boundaries. In the forests they just put marks on the trees to separate their woods."

48

She could have been describing life here ten years ago rather than a thousand. To me everything about Deseşti looked medieval.

"In the 1930s, the large estates were broken up to give more land to small-holders..." I smiled encouragingly: surely that had been a good move? "...It was fine until people realised that Romanian inheritance laws don't include the right of primogeniture. Land and properties are divided between male and female children. If a daughter marries a rich man, her dowry would be equal to that of her brothers' shares. Let's say we are talking about a family of five children, three sons and two daughters. Maybe they have five hectares. In that case the youngest son stays with his parents and inherits the household and the tools; the two other sons are allowed to have homes on the land."

"And the girls?"

"Well, the girls would get nothing until they married, but then they would inherit one hectare each, as well as cattle to the value of their land and things for their household. That's why the landholdings are getting smaller and smaller and less and less profitable."

Now I understood why some Maramureş villages have kept the practice of endogamy and why they do not like 'strangers'. In this case a stranger does not mean a person from a foreign country but anyone from another village.

Paşa had a wealth of knowledge about local plants. She made what she called a digestive tea from a mixture of herbs that grew in her garden. Then she gave me some beauty tips, Maramureş style. It must have been clear to her by now that I did not go around with a handbag full of face powder and lipsticks, or indeed a handbag. Sometimes I caught a glance of something that was not exactly disdain, but more like concern over my weird behaviour. I had not progressed as far as a pair of Doctor Marten's bovver boots, but in the year or two before Romania, now that it was safe to be Punk, I had been trying to find an identity in London's counter culture, ending up with a look that was something between county and grunge. Possibly this suggestion that we should *nous soigner* was Paşa's way of being tactful. It seemed horribly middle-aged to me.

It would have been churlish to refuse. Anyway, what she was going to show me might have scientific interest. It turned out to be fun and, by the standards of the green movement, positively glowing with environmental benefits. Beside the hedge outside her gate was a plant with long, serrated leaves, like a giant dandelion but softer and slightly hairy to the touch. She picked about a dozen of the leaves and brought them onto the verandah. Then she chose a wide enamelled bowl from a stack in the kitchen and put the leaves inside. Then she poured boiling water over them.

"Now we leave them to cool," she said, enjoying this moment of girl talk, "and when it's ready, you will see, this is a wonderful way to clean your face."

It was true: when I splashed the pale green liquid, still warm, over my face, it left it feeling wonderfully soft. Eat your heart out, Fairy Liquid. Paşa's hints included another recipe that involved placing the flowers of a lily into a bottle with some alcohol; she swore that this was a sure-fire method of removing skin blemishes and sun-spots. Somehow I could not imagine doing that at home. Where would I find wild lilies in Cricklewood?

Men and mushrooms

Early one morning we went searching for mushrooms in the rough pastures above Deseşti. Paşa's husband came too, but stayed a little apart from us. He looked embarrassed to be out so early in the morning, and with women at that. Her nephew's little dog came with us more willingly. He had an English name, Blackie, and spent most of his time tied to a bench in her brother's garden.

It was five o'clock and the sun was still rising as we climbed through farmyards and orchards. We made shortcuts where we could. Gradually the lanes became footpaths and finally metamorphosed into the beds of streams where we had to hop from one boulder to another. Stopping to catch my breath, I looked to where the sky was brightest; it was in the direction of Ukraine. All I could see was row upon row of mountain peaks. The valleys between them were brimming with mist.

We walked on, panting with the effort, until we reached the upper slopes of the hill behind Deseşti. It was glorious to be up so early and hunting for food. Then the serious work began. Paşa was in her element and as focussed as a truffle hound. She darted from tree to gully, and from piles of pungent leaves to bristly thickets, calling out "Voilà, quels jolis champignons!" each time she found a new hoard. Then she would slice them expertly from the ground with a kitchen knife. They came in all shapes, from frilly yellow to phallic pink and white, from tiny closed cups to the flatness and width of a dinner plate. Paşa tried to teach me the difference between the edible and the poisonous ones. I tried to listen, but I knew that on my own it would be impossible.

Before going back to her house for breakfast we picked tiny, sweet, wild raspberries and purple myrtle berries with the bloom still on them. We were in a landscape that was orchard, open heath and forest. On the way down, it started to rain.

"Did you know that people used to find water from the ends of rainbows?" Paşa asked. I shook my head, bemused, thinking it might be a joke. "They would look for the place where the rainbow fell to earth, and they would find water there. They used to dowse too. Another way was to find the kind of plants that like a lot of water: you can be pretty sure to discover a source there too. We can dry off in here."

We had stopped outside a small shed. The door opened and a blast of violent heat smacked us in the face. Inside we found a copper furnace, some elaborate piping, and a man with a face as red as a ripe cherry. The hut was a still for making plum brandy which Romanians call 'ţuica' or 'horinca', depending on its strength. We each had a tot; it was razor sharp and shot down into my stomach like a bullet. Stills are not illegal in Romania and you can find them everywhere, varying architecturally from shacks to fine brick buildings. They are often communal, and during the early autumn when the fruit is ready for distilling they become social gathering points. In another Maramureş village I went to, the still was known as the language factory. This was because once you had drunk a few glasses you could speak any tongue on earth. In nearby Slătioara, a retired teacher had mechanised the still, ensuring that the all-important stirring process went at the right speed.

Paşa cooked the mushrooms, placing some of them whole on the top of her wood-fired cooking stove and the rest in a large, shallow frying pan after heating some oil; then she added onions, salt and eggs. They tasted fantastic.

The secret folklorist

After we had eaten, we sat on the verandah looking out over the yard.

"You know, it's odd about the way things are going," Paşa said. "Now we have the beginnings of democracy, but we have got so used to being told what to do, we can't handle it. But there was a real tradition of democracy here once, although no-one outside knows about it any more. These villages worked like a closed unit. There was a natural economy in which most of our needs were fulfilled locally, and what's more, everyone showed great respect for the elders. We had something called 'devălmaş', where the father of a family was more like a boss of a firm. His children were his team, but they were also like individual proprietors. It wasn't as though the people were sedentary or inward-looking either. In the time before the feudal Hungarian lords, country people would travel long distances to communicate and trade with each other. So instead of isolated centres, all the communities within Maramureş, and some outside it too, were linked.

"People from different regions came together to exchange goods, and fairs were organised for this; these fairs were also held for religious and social reasons. The most important ones were the 'nedei'; these were annual events that were held on top of the mountains. It meant that people living on both sides could meet at least once a year. Of course it was a chance for shepherds to find wives: that's the origin of the famous Girl Fair on Mt. Găina..." - this mountain is in the Apuseni range to the west of Cluj - "...It was the one time in their lives that young people could meet each other without their parents keeping an eye on them, and sometimes they would get married. I've seen photos from the 1930s showing girls hiking up the mountain sides in crocodile formation, each one with her pack pony. We had something like it here in Maramureş, in fact it still exists." She smiled at the reminiscence. "It's called 'Ispas'. Occasionally the boys and girls who meet there end up by getting married."

"But the Girl Fair isn't a marriage market any more, is it?" I asked.

"No, it has become an excuse for an open air party; there are stalls selling all kinds of trashy goods, and bands who play traditional music. It's quite fun, but the whole thing has become very commercial."

It was confusing: on the one hand, Maramureş villages had a strong sense of self-ownership and 'kept themselves to themselves'. There was a conviction that the mountains and the forests were a refuge; one of the most often repeated sayings is, 'the forest is the Romanian's friend'. A lot of folklore attached to the safe-keeping of villages: painted crucifixes were placed at cross-roads and at the entrances to villages, because people thought evil spirits lurked there. Sometimes the boundaries were protected by fountains or other magic signs which a contemporary traveller would pass without noticing. On the other hand, I knew from my own experience that people were hospitable and curious for information. They were far from stupid, illiterate peasants: in its time Maramureş had produced a lot of intellectuals. I remembered being told that one of the first books written in Romanian, in Cyrillic characters, had been found in the region's oldest shrine, the 14th century wooden church in Ieud. This was the 'Zbornicul de la Ieud', a book of laws and cooking recipes which had been found in the choir gallery.

In 1974 Ceauşescu made a speech in the Maramureş urging Romanians to preserve the customs of their forefathers. Soon afterwards he initiated 'Cântarea al României', or the Song to Romania, a biennial arts festival that featured competitions of folk music and dance. It was designed to glorify Ceauşescu as The Nation's Greatest Son, and the performances culminated in mass displays of loyal devotion. Taking part in this exhibition was obligatory if you wanted to keep your job. It was a sycophantic exercise and diluted the country's gutsy art forms. But I wondered if in some ways, The Song to Romania might also have helped to keep those traditions alive. I had to be sceptical; although they had preserved some elements of Romania's folk culture, by and large the communists had twisted its spirit into a kitsch and sterile travesty.

I felt sure that the communists' attempts to ban ancient rituals had not succeeded in Maramureş. I was longing for Paşa to enlighten me. What did people believe? And how did they apply these beliefs to their daily lives? Paşa went inside and returned with two huge bundles of buff-coloured files.

"Look," she said, "this is what I did to keep myself sane during the Ceauşescu years. It was not allowed of course – I had to keep it secret, but I collected stories from the old people in our villages, not just in Deseşti but from neighbouring ones as well. I've got eighteen like these. I'm hoping to publish them some day." I could not wait to see them. Paşa dumped the files on her desk and handed me one. Even if my Romanian had been good enough to read it, the irregular blue typewriting had faded so that I could hardly make them out. I felt as though I were handling a rare and priceless document. Instead I demanded more examples, and Paşa seemed happy to oblige.

"If a child became ill, its mother would 'sell' it to another woman from another village, or she would change its name – you could see notices on people's windows announcing a child for sale," she said. I looked shocked. "Yes, it's true; it was supposed to cure the child – she didn't really give it away! And it was bad luck if a father chose where his own child's cot should go. Better that a stranger should do it."

"And does this still happen?"

"Oh yes, absolutely," she replied.

Paşa worked hard all day long, in the house, on her mother's farm and at school. I did not know how much it was costing her to talk to me like this but I wanted to know what she thought: of women's lives in present-day Romania, of the legends she had so painstakingly collected, of the outside world, of politics and freedom, of market economies and how small communities could survive. After our mushroom feast, she let me interview her, and I recorded her comments while we sat on a rug near the plum trees.

The chickens made comforting, harmonious noises in the background, as though endorsing their mistress's words.

"I think feminism is a kind of luxury for women in the west; they have the freedom to allow themselves all kinds of ideas," she said. "Women here have been totally ignored since the Revolution: before there was a chance for a woman to get on, but now..." Her voice trailed away with a tinge of resentment.

"What would you like to see happen in the future?" I enquired.

"I would like to see women able to spend time on themselves..." - she used the French 'se soigner' - "...and to have the chance to study and make something of their lives. Society has a duty to protect women, no? After all, women are the mothers of humanity; they used to be the chiefs. In this area it is a custom that unmarried and married women wear different clothes, they become more sombre when they are married, and the old women, many of whom are widows, always wear black. Things are changing but there are still certain rules about behaviour. Women do not walk alone in the streets at night, or go to a restaurant on their own, and they never visit a man in his house if they are alone."

Paşa returned to her criticism of Romanian men.

"They do not look after their wives well enough; they impose on them the 'traditional' life of a woman, which dictates that a wife must not only do all the housework and give birth and bring up her children, but also go out to work. She has no time or energy to develop her mind." There was a short pause, then she continued more philosophically: "I don't think it is possible to make men and women equal. We are different from the moment we are born. Men are more egotistic and they have more courage than women. Women are more sensitive and complex; they assume more responsibilities and duties. And perhaps they are more intelligent, too... Men don't want women to be equal to them; their masculine pride suffers when a woman does better than them. That's why they put such a lot of pressure on us to work; they are scared of letting us have our freedom in case we beat them. They love us but they don't love us at the same time; they need us, that's all..." She dissolved into laughter. "What would my husband say if he could hear me now! "

For a while neither of us spoke as we contemplated the bewildering network of continually renegotiated relationships that kept the world together, or tore it apart, according to your point of view. Later she admitted,

"Men here have to work hard, too; they have jobs in the forests or in the mines, and when they come home they are exhausted, but some of them help their wives at home. You can't imagine how hard life is here: before 1989 the villagers could afford to buy bread from the village bakery and they had tractors. Now, bread has shot up in price and the tractors have disappeared." This story about the mysteriously vanishing tractors was something I had heard before; the unspoken accusation was that security officers had sold them off on the black market, leaving the unfortunate small holders to work their land with horses and oxen as best they could.

Paşa smiled again, and, returning to a favourite subject:

"We have other customs that I like very much. Mothers sing to their children a lot. That is why the children here are so bonny. They are never sent to bed unhappy even when they have been very naughty; my mother always sang to me when I was a child".

If it sounded a bit sentimental, I had to agree that the children I had seen in Maramureş were happy and good-looking; they seemed to be laughing all the time. Their faces were so different from the petrified masks of the diseased and starving orphans which bombarded our television screens after Ceauşescu was shot.

As if to convince me, Paşa started singing:

"Haia, liulea puişor,
Te culca mama cu dor.
Haia, liulea, pui de peşte,
Eu te leagan, şi tu-i creşte
Haia liulea, pui de cuc,
Eu te leagan, şi mă duc.
De-oi pute cumva lucra,
De nu ţi-i tare canta"

('Come my pretty little dove,
Mummy will put you to bed with love.
Come my little wriggly fry,
I will rock you and you'll grow high
Come my little cuckoo chick,
I will rock you, then I'm leaving quick.
If you could use your energy up
Then you wouldn't want to sing so much.')

At last, Paşa started talking about the myths she had collected.

"There are so many categories: myths about the forest and the night, about the wind, the rain and the sun, there are myths about the roads and the flowers, the trees and the mountains, about the lakes and water, and of the fields. They embody a kind of morality which is very old but also very modern at the same time. You have seen what the people are like in this village: they are open-hearted and simple, but they think deeply too. Nobody steals; we don't have any crime here to speak of. Everyone's door is open.

55

People care about the traditional customs and they look after their festival clothes and pass them on down the generations. Maybe these things have survived here because we are surrounded by mountains and progress has passed us by. Of course the old beliefs are disappearing now.

"You've seen the carpet in my room? It has some very old designs on it. They are geometric abstractions taken from the idea of the tree of life. And there are other ancient patterns which weavers here use, like the round dance. That goes back to a Neolithic hunters' dance, something they did to encourage prosperity, conserve human energies and collect the forces of the universe." I had seen some rugs from Maramureş patterned with alternating male and female figures who were holding hands, but Paşa was adding other examples to her theme. "Another very common motif is the wave, which encompasses everything." I thought of Brâncuşi's columns, and of the zigzag forms and patterns that were popular here. I had seen them on farm gates, around the bodies of churches, and bordering little cups like the ones we had bought from Petru Pop a Niţu in Breb.

"My favourite myths are the ones about Fata Pădurii (the girl of the forest) and Omul Nopţii (the man of the night), the little beauty who is the goddess of the wind, and what else...?" She broke off, either thinking or hesitating. I wondered if Paşa was reluctant to say more before she published her research. Presently the moment of doubt or reflection passed, and she continued, "...Well, there are so many..." - and she reeled off a few names: Marţolea, Slăbănogele, Frumuşelele, Şolomonarii; fairies, witches and trolls, I supposed, none of which I had ever heard of before.

The Girl of the Forest and the Man of the Night

"The Girl of the Forest is my favourite, but I've never spoken about her much to anyone. She is not unique to Romania, but she has a very special rôle here, particularly in Maramureş. I found lots of stories about her. She is a great ecologist! She claims that there are places on the Earth which belong to her alone where no man must enter. If he does, she punishes him. Fata Pădurii is feminine and always very beautiful, but she is also extremely bad. She lives in the forests, on the tops of mountains, in rare flowers, in medicinal plants and in mineral water; she can also be found in certain special rocks - in any place, in fact, which must be kept safe from man. She is the spirit that inhabits the rains and the storms. Fata Pădurii gets close to men rather than women, because men tend to explore further from their homes, and they are the ones who climb the mountains. Shepherds and woodcutters are at the most risk from her attentions. She sets certain rules for them: shepherds must not bring their lovers to the sheepfold; they mustn't visit them in the valleys either, nor even think about them when they are working in the fold." Paşa broke off to take several puffs from her cigarette.

"This rule meant the shepherds must stay celibate from St. George's Day (24th April) right through to the autumn, because in Romania's mountain areas they use the ancient system of moving sheep between winter and summer pastures, and the flocks have to be watched all the time - literally twenty-four hours a day - in case a wolf or a bear attacks them. If they don't obey her, Fata Pădurii adopts their lovers' shape and visits them. Instead of making love as they expect, she turns into a sadist: she beats them up and drags them over the rocks by their hair. She practically kills them; in fact, sometimes she does kill them! The men who survive carry the scars ever afterwards: some of them have paralysed faces, others get epilepsy. Fata Pădurii can take other shapes as well: a horse, the wind, or a foreign woman, but she is always lovely to look at. She has a little garden on a mountain top where she grows gorgeous flowers. No-one must pick her flowers unless they leave something in exchange: a lump of cheese, some eggs or a lot of money. Sometimes she has children; they are always ugly and hairy. She has another rule: mothers mustn't leave their babies on their own. If they do, Fata Pădurii will steal the baby; if it's a beautiful little boy, she exchanges him for an ugly one."

It was a breathtaking image with threads of Greek mythology woven into old wives' tales and stories you could read in James Frazer's 'The Golden Bough'. From where we were sitting, in the heart of some of Europe's loveliest countryside, it was highly seductive. Paşa added:

"The majority of stories about Fata Pădurii show her in a bad light, but I don't think she was always bad. In fact I can prove that she was as good as she was bad. But in order to find her positive side..." - Paşa used the term 'iubirea ei sălbatică' ('her wild form of love') - "...men must understand what she is trying to teach them. They have to conduct themselves according to the norms imposed by her ancient philosophy." Paşa chose the word 'om', meaning 'person' in its masculine sense, quite deliberately. In her eyes, males posed the greatest threat to the environment, and I knew from my reading that Maramureş was a place where females had been in the ascendant. It was a long time ago, before the Indo-Europeans migrated here from Central Asia some five to seven thousand years before Christ. Those mysterious women were much in feminists' minds. I had read something about them in books by Marija Gimbu-

tas and Naomi Mitchison. Neither of us said it, but I guessed that both of us felt it was a shame the age had passed.

We took up the mythological theme the next day. Paşa described the character she called the Man of the Night: she said he was exclusive to Maramureş, and existed as Fata Pădurii's minder. Ill-favoured, hirsute, but good by nature, he followed her around, keeping an eye on her and intervening when she became too savage. Sometimes he killed her to prevent her from taking control of the entire world.

"The Man of the Night looks after the shepherds, and takes care of the roads, and occasionally he guards the front doors of houses.

"There are lots of explanations as to who these characters are, and lots of stories connected with each one; I'm sure you could find books which contradict what I've told you, showing the same characters from a completely different angle. But what's interesting is that these myths still exist in the midst of a technological age. Young people and children know them too, but of course it's the old who are most familiar with them, and they tell them again, day after day. I started collecting these stories when I was a student. I did my degree on the mythology of the Maramureş. My professor was Mihai Pop and he encouraged me to carry on, even though everybody on the academic advisory board knew that these things were regarded as superstitions and were forbidden."

I asked her if her decision to study this subject was a form of personal resistance to the communist regime.

"Yes, it was; life under the communists was unbearable. It was very hard; I often nearly gave up – but then I remembered how important these myths are, not only to Romanians, but to people outside as well. I spent all my spare time doing the research, I used my own money and I worked in secret, doing field trips during the university holidays. People would ask me what on earth I was doing. I would answer, it's OK, I'm working on the land, that's all, nothing else – just a countrywoman cultivating the earth." She made it sound positively elemental. "Sometimes friends from France or England would bring me books on mythology, and I read Mircea Eliade, the great religious historian whose work was banned here until 1981. A state publishing house printed the first volume of his 'A History of Religious Ideas' in that year. Up till then I could only read his work in a special section of the Academy library; Professor Pop had to get me a permit!"

Paşa explained something else:

"I had a little cousin who used to come and stay with us. She used to beg me to tell her stories about the girl from the wood. She didn't want the same ones over and over again. So I asked my father, my neighbours, and other old people to tell me their versions of the myth. They persuaded me to write them down in case they should get lost and eventually I realised something incredible: each story brings something new and specific to the legend. While I was working on this research I developed a sort of archaeological method, 'des petites morceaux on fait un pot'! Now I have 500 texts and the problem is knowing where to stop. The subject is inexhaustible."

Paşa got up to collect some of the ripe plums that now and then thudded damply onto the grass, and brought them back for us to share.

"I have left these stories exactly as I heard them, only making some additional comments and notes. You know, it is very unusual for these stories to survive intact. It is my small contribution. And do you know what? Sometimes I find that ideas in the stories about space and time are being expressed by the most advanced modern physicists! It's strange!"

Paşa made light of her work, but I knew she felt deeply about it. She had lost her father whom she adored; her marriage was on the rocks, she had no children, and her mother needed constant attention. The fairy stories that Paşa had told me occupy a different world from that of politics, but they reminded me of Jean Giraudoux's Mad Woman of Chaillot, who wrecks the global stock exchange because she believes it is destroying the natural order of things.

We talked about the potential for developing medicinal and cosmetic plants in Maramureş. Both of us knew that it would take far more than our combined expertise to produce them in enough quantities to be economically viable, at least in the terms that the financial manager of a modern company would recognise. To save the plants and the knowledge that went with them you would have to transform the countryside, or large parts of it, into industrial processing plants, using chemical fertilisers and preservatives, with scores of greenhouses and everything arranged in orderly rows. We were both sure there must be another way that was less environmentally and aesthetically devastating but equally productive. A collection of cottagers who would cultivate and process different plants in his or her handkerchief of a backgarden? Or could the plants be harvested wild? Who would do the marketing? Who would take such an approach seriously? Who would make sure that the producers were the ones to benefit most? Those were some of the issues that stayed hanging in the air. They still are.

Wild mushrooms have become big business for the Maramureş. I watched as Deseşti's piece workers brought the harvest in one evening. At the packer's barn, tired old men and women and boisterous children queued to empty the contents of plastic bags, cardboard boxes and nylon carriers into weighing dishes. Then, all their effort expended and looking slightly deflated, they turned away gratefully counting wads of 'lei' that would hardly buy one of the mushrooms they had picked by the time they reached the expensive restaurants in Milan. Paşa knew the packer and his family; she introduced me to his daughter. She was eight years old and her father had just given her a wild fawn for a pet. Deer and child were about the same size. The fawn looked lost in its makeshift cage and the little girl fussed over it as though it were a doll.

Paşa's sister-in-law Victoria gave me my first taste of 'mamaliga'. This is the most traditional of Romanian foods, a bright yellow polenta that you boil for hours and then leave to set into a thick cake. Mamaliga is a meal in itself - Romanians eat it with sour cream or cream cheese – but, stodgy as it sounds, it is delicious with seafood and a salad; it is supposed to prolong your life for decades.

One afternoon I passed a funeral cortege making its way up the hill to Sfa Paraschiva. A line of men and women in black and white straggled behind a coffin on a cart. They were mostly old people; they sang a dirge as they walked. Then suddenly an old lady shouted a phrase at the top of her voice, repeating it several times. The sound made my hair stand on end. The coffin was open and a face as transparent as cameo glass stared blankly at the sky. Paşa said:

"When my father died, his body was carried on a cart drawn by four oxen". Her eyes filled with tears. It had happened last year.

It was time to leave Deseşti. Paşa had to return to a teaching job in Baia Mare and I was hunting for something that was as elusive as the deer: a way of avoiding the total collapse of Romania's traditional culture, of maintaining small communities at a level of prosperity that they could sustain without letting them disappear into the maw of international corporations who were only interested in them as potential consumers-for-life.

It was paradoxical: Romania was terribly poor but as Paşa had said, 'we are rich in spirit'. She had meant the Maramureş, and what she told me bore the imprint of her religious faith. I was more sceptical by nature, but there was something in this country that had taken hold of me and would not let go.

3

Valley hopping

If you take the road north from Deseşti you come to the village of Hărniceşti. I got off there to talk to a young teacher whose name Paşa had given me. He had revived a custom that dates back to Roman times. It was called 'Tânjaua' and was held in May to celebrate the arrival of the growing season. Tânjaua ('Tuehnjower' is the closest I can get to an accurate pronunciation) is also a competition designed to encourage young men to plough the first furrow. The winner claims the title of most industrious farmer for the year ahead. But first he has to be chased and caught by the other young men of the village. At the same time, the men parade through the village with a ceremonial plough made of branches and decorated with ribbons, streamers and fronds of spruce.

On the day of the procession everyone puts on their traditional finery. The women wear embroidered blouses, white petticoats and striped woollen aprons, and the men put on long white shirts and white wool or linen trousers, topping the ensemble with a 'clop'.

After a hectic chase the star of the show must be carried over a cross made of salt on the threshold of his house and then provide his captors with a good lunch. Then everyone lets their hair down. Most of the young people end up larking about in the river. The rest of the day is abandoned to eating, drinking, singing and dancing.

The custom had continued in other villages during the communist period, but in Hărniceşti it virtually disappeared until 1995. The young man who revived it told me that the custom had remained in the collective folk memory and the young and old had picked it up as though there had been no break at all.

"Maramureş has always been special," he explained. "The communities here are very proud of their cultural heritage and to them, making Tânjaua again was a way of wiping out the bad years in between."

Five years later, he had left Romania and the custom died out in Hărniceşti as quickly as it had been revived. Quietly and inevitably, Europe had lost another of its treasures. But I was lucky: Tânjaua had survived in Hoteni, a few miles from here. Hoteni was the home of a pair of folksingers whose names were famous across Romania: Georgeta and Ioan Pop. Even though it was the wrong time of year for celebrating the plough, I decided to go there to find them.

I got a lift with a man and his wife in a battered Dacia; they were working as engineers on a hydro-electric plant in Peru and had come home for a holiday; the Dacia belonged to a cousin. I asked the man if he knew the Pops. He banged the steering wheel in triumph.

"That's incredible! You know our famous singers too?"

We drove over a rise and a new valley opened out before us. If anything it was more pastoral than the one we had left because we were a little further from civilisation and the Baia Mare road. The landscape was open and flowed away from us on all sides, rising slightly to high ground a few miles away with no hedges to block the view. It was mostly grassland with patches of strip farming. In the distance the hillsides were contoured with terracing. As we approached Hoteni, there were wooden houses set back from the road in the middle of orchards on either side. One of them, noticeable for the work that was going on there, belonged to the Pops.

Geta Pop was one of four sisters who had been born on a farm in Hoteni. Her parents were elderly and sick, and she and her siblings did what they could to help them keep the farm running. Geta's husband, Ion, was known as Popica. He sang with an English folk band called Popeluc, but also had his own group, Iza, which was named after the Valley where they lived.

Ce rău am fă - cut la lu - me - - - - -, Ce rău am fă-
cut la lu - me -, De nu - mi-aud vor - be bu - ne,
De nu mi-aud vor - be bu - - ne - - - - -.

('What evil have I done to the world/That I hear no good words said of me?'...)

I had heard this exquisitely mournful song in recordings, and here it was again as a live performance by Geta Pop as she gathered clothes from the washing line.

Geta was as slender and springy as a Maramureş pitchfork. She regarded me with frank amusement.

"So you are wandering around looking for signs of our cultural history? You can stay here for a night, but you will have to share a room with my mother, my sister and me. That will be a cultural experience for you!"

It was cold again, and the farmhouse stove had been going all day. After making a dash for the outside lavatory and sluicing my teeth, I climbed into a massive bed with pillows made of concrete and pulled the sheets right over my head. Geta's mother coughed through the night; she looked deathly pale and it was a relief to all of us that she made it safely alive to the morning. By seven a.m. the daughters were busying themselves in the kitchen, which was housed in a shed next to the house. One side was completely open and it was freezing in there. We had warm milk straight from the cow, fresh bread and cold, spicy sausage.

"Next time, you can stay in our house," said Geta, and before I left we walked down the hill to the superb wooden cabin which she and Popica had rescued and were now restoring. "And you can bring me an English rose," she added, "I would like to have one here in my garden."

There is a video of Geta and Popica performing a dashing duet in which each singer hurls abuse at the other in a classic male-female battle. It was made in the parlour of somebody's house one evening after Tânjaua, and the couple and their audience are dressed up in their traditional finery. At home among their friends and neighbours, the singers' flying insults have a bite that no staged drama could equal.

I will lie with the sun, the stars and the moon

Back on the Mara valley road again, I went north to Berbeşti. From the highway it is a village like any other, but beside the road at the north end of the village was a covered wooden cross. It incorporated an anthropomorphic image of the sun and moon, and on the ground below it the figures of St. John and Mary Magdalene clustered protectively around a Virgin and Child. The cross was made in the early 18th century by serfs who were tied to the land. Now it was rickety and battered. If I had not been told about it first I might not have given it a second glance. And yet the mark of potent, ancient beliefs was still on it, as though some quirk of fate had failed to sweep it away, like Romania itself.

There were moments of anxiety when I feared the beauty of Maramureş would vanish before my eyes. In these moments it was as fragile as a body that has been preserved in a vacuum; once someone punctures it, the body falls to dust. I knew there were people who felt like me, and for that reason they kept the place a secret.

65

It was a dilemma: should I stay quiet and not write about it, or write about it and share the treasure with others? I knew a writer who was exporting the wooden houses to museums in western Europe. He argued that it was the only way of saving them for posterity. Most people here were too poor to worry about such things; they put their precious embroideries on their fences hoping that a passing foreigner would snap them up. Since the Revolution a great deal of evaporation had already taken place; but there were people who had set their minds on putting a lid on further loss: here and there, projects designed to promote and develop skills in traditional crafts were blossoming. I did not know if my attitude was realistic: my feelings said yes but my cynical head said no. There was a debate going on inside me as I stumped along. Which was more important: my pleasure as a tourist or the well-being of thousands of people? Was it selfish of me to want Maramureş to stay where it was? But in fact I did not want it to stay where it was, only that it should go forward in a way that did not destroy what was already good – and what the West had lost.

I was on my way to the Cosău Valley, where one of the self-help projects I had heard about was in progress. The Mara and Cosău rivers merge at Berbeşti and all I had to do was turn left at the fork near the cross. Cosău is one of the four valleys that comprise 'historic' Maramureş, where old customs had survived the best. Villages in the valley have joined forces to promote their culture and tourism. They have won a grant from the Carpathian Foundation and the King Baudouin Fund in Belgium. Slowly and imperceptibly the idea of self-help has taken root here. It has given the people a sense of hope and self-respect. The dreaded word 'collective' has not passed anyone's lips, but the villagers are cooperating in a way that would not have been possible under communism.

I was walking through a landscape that had evolved so differently from the part of Oxfordshire where I grew up. It was not wild; people had managed it for millenia. But the management was unobtrusive. It was pointless to compare this area with what passes for open country in Britain. Inevitably, though, I did compare it: Maramureş looked medieval but was truly lived in, while the British national parks tried to maintain 'traditional' land use and architecture with half-hearted results. Old stone cottages that could have been restored to house local young people on the Preseli Hills were left to ruin because they were picturesque. Here the old wooden buildings fell into ruin because no-one could afford to mend them. Agriculture here was 'low impact' and organic, not out of choice but necessity. Collectivisation had not reached very far into the Maramureş. This had allowed people to carry on farming by the old methods. You could tell the difference in the way that people regarded the land. Where there had been continuity in farming, there was a sense of purpose and strength. It showed in people's faces and in the cultivation of the land. Where collectivisation had broken the old village communities, along the edges of Maramureş, agriculture had suffered.

Below the sharp mountain ridges, the land was softer, rounded and green. Shallow terracing articulated the hillsides and haystacks punctuated them. There were no great highways and cars shared the asphalt of the roads that existed with slow-moving carts. It was not an idyllic landscape. Signs of poverty were visible in the broken-down houses and rusting farm equipment. People here had learnt to make do and mend. But their poverty was not abject and their 'old ways' were not useless. Viable alternatives to modern farming methods exist. It needs the political imagination and will to understand their qualities.

Ladders of Virtue; Stairs from Hell

About 12 kms south from the Berbeşti turn lies the village of Călineşti. On the way the view changed. The outlines of the mountains changed, reinforcing the sensation that this was a real place, not a dream. To the south and east I could see the Lăpuş and Ţibleş ranges. Gentler foothills rose in between; in Romanian they are called 'piemonţi' (as in Italian 'piedmonts'), and their slopes were sprinkled with haystacks. These haystacks fascinated me: in Romania they can be as expressive as a Rodin sculpture. I have seen them leaning together in family groups, marching down a pasture in soldierly rows, and standing alone as though in meditation. To keep the hay dry, it is occasionally stored on a low, square platform which has a movable roof. This gives the impression of a hat. In winter the haystacks give off heat and you can see steam curling out of them.

It was sometimes lonely on the road that summer; the chance to talk was reduced by the language barrier. In contrast I felt safer than I did in London and adjusted easily to the new pace of life. Two legs suited me fine. I did not want to charge around in a car disturbing the peace. The atmosphere was alive with interesting sounds. Wherever I went there was an orchestra of unconscious musicians. Bee-eaters tootled in the acacias and woodpeckers tapped for grubs; cattle bellowed mournfully, and even on the remotest hilltops, the sound of barking floated up to me. Trotting horses, somebody hammering on wood, the occasional shout, the wind rustling through leaves, water rushing over pebbles; if I was at a loss socially my senses were never alone.

There are two wooden churches in Călineşti, and the oldest is a former monastery. It is very small and hugs a steep hillside on one edge of the village, half-hidden behind tall fir trees. Nobody holds services here any more. The building is an historic monument and has a neglected feeling. I wondered how long it would survive. When monks lived here they would open the west door and allow parishioners a view of the icon screen. There was so little space inside the church that villagers had to worship in the porch. It is a beautiful porch, large enough to hold twenty or thirty people. The guardian unlocked a side door and I bent down so as not to bang my head on the lintel.

Inside all the walls had been painted in fresco. Georgeta Iuga had told me there was a rare example here of a scene called the Ladder of Virtue. It was in the pronaos. When I found it I let out a "Wow!"

The theme goes way back in religious history. It must be connected to the story of Jacob's Ladder, but here it originates in the writings of a 7th century monk from Mt. Sinai. The symbolism is simple: if you want to get to Heaven you must make the effort to climb up to it, and climbing implies trying to become a better person. In this composition, monks try to enter Paradise by ascending a ladder with thirty-three rungs. Each rung represents a year of Christ's life, but it also stands for a particular virtue. The monks have to prove that they have the virtue before they can climb further up the ladder. At the top, Christ leans out of the window of Heaven ready to embrace anyone who makes the grade. I knew there were other versions of the scene in Romania but they were in the grander monasteries to the east. I had never heard of one in such a little shrine, nor so far into the west. St. John Climacos of St. Catherine's Monastery in Sinai put the idea into writing in the 600s; as far as I knew the first illustration of the theme was a 12th century icon in St. Catherine's. The Ladder appeared most often in illuminated manuscripts, but there were fresco versions in Balkan monasteries, and on Mt. Athos.

The painting in Călineşti's wooden monastery had been done in the 18th century. It was crude but remarkably fresh, even though the church was damp. The colours and the drawing of the figures had held their strength.

The painting made me wonder again about the relationship between Orthodox and Greco-Catholics in this area. Who cared about this little building, and what did it mean to the people here? Orthodoxy had returned to Maramureş during a programme of forced re-conversions which was carried out in the 1950s. A population which had grown accustomed to the Greco-Catholic rite now had to change back to the Byzantine one because of an agreement between the Romanian Patriarch and the communist government. Henceforth Orthodoxy became the official national religion. In every parish churchyard long lines of villagers walked past a committee consisting of local party officials and an Orthodox priest who sat looking at them from behind a table set up for the purpose of conversion. One can imagine the stony, impassive faces. Since 1989 the tables have turned again. Greco-Catholicism is no longer outlawed, and the former Greco-Catholics want their churches back. Sadly the Orthodox authorities have not always been as ready to give as they were to receive. Because of this an unseemly struggle is going on between two branches of the Christian church.

On my way up the hill from the monastery I passed an orchard in which someone had built an outdoor oven out of clay bricks. It stood about four feet high and had a pitched roof which made it look like a large dolls' house. I liked the way that cart wheels, yokes, boards from winter sleighs, harrows and ploughs and wooden forks had been hung on the walls of the farm barns to keep them tidily out of the way. They looked like a frieze.

There was hardly any motor traffic and only one asphalt road through the village. When a car did bluster through it annoyed me. Occasionally someone went by on a bicycle. One farmstead abutted the next and each one had its tall gate; some of the gates were leaning drunkenly outwards in their frames. Wood is appealing even when rotting. I tried to imagine the houses with metal fences and plastic gates. The thought made me shudder.

"Do Mr and Mrs Berindei live here?" I had knocked on the glass door on one side of a neat courtyard in the middle of Călineşti. When it opened a smiling woman appeared, quickly followed by a smiling man. We agreed a price and I was settled for another night.

On the other side of the yard was a new house which had been built specially for tourists. It was a two-storey breeze block building enclosed in a small garden. There was an old tractor in the yard; it did not work any more but had been converted ingeniously into a mobile saw-bench. At the back, the driveway sloped downhill to a dog kennel. Its occupant slavered viciously at me everytime I went to the lavatory which stood opposite his kennel; it was a shed hung out over the midden next to the pigsty.

I had the guest house to myself that night and slept in isolated grandeur. The Berindeis stayed on the other side of the yard in a chalet-style cabin. I ate supper with them; we had home-made sausages, pickled sweet peppers and fresh bread. Afterwards, my hosts and I drank beer together companionably on the first floor balcony. As the sun started to go down, the air was rent with hideous screams. The family pig was being mated in the yard. A hulking boar had been led into the yard by a ring in his nose, and while he was preoccupied at one end, my hostess's mother, determined to get her money's worth, had caught hold of the unfortunate sow's ears with both hands and was holding on like grim death at the other. An audience of fascinated faces peered over the gate, watching the proceedings from the safety of the street and shouting encouragement.

Sometime later I drifted off to the piteous howls of the guard-dog in his cage; clearly everyone had been moved by the evening's events. An exotic décor of glittery purple and green and pink covered the walls and ceiling of my room. The combination of violently clashing colours and glitter was guaranteed to give me nightmares. There was a shiny velvet picture of a stag hunt on one wall. Outside my door a plastic tree-rose stood in a tub complete with full, pink blooms. The only thing which did not grate on the eye was the stair carpet, which had obviously been woven specially for the house: it was made of soft, undyed sheep's wool with a discreet linear pattern in dark red. It was a beautiful piece of work, and showed off the natural black, brown and grey colours to perfection. Getting up to go to the outside loo in the night, I nearly broke my neck because it was lying loose on the stairs.

Sârbi's Beautiful Launderette

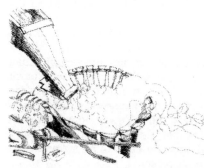

Sârbi lies beyond Călineşti; when I try to pronounce it, its name sounds like a chirrup. If you go there on a Friday you can see the whirlpool which is the village launderette. These devices are designed for washing clothes and blankets and for fulling textiles. The whirlpools are constructed in the open. They work by diverting a stream through a series of narrow channels so that it is forced at hgh speed into a wooden bowl. The sides of the bowl are made of wooden slats which splay out in a fan shape and are tied together with willow stems, rope or wire. The waste water flows back into the stream through the gaps between the slats. Romanians call these washtubs 'vâltori'. Sârbi's vâltoare belonged to one particular household but it was opened once a week so that other housewives in the village could bring their washing to the yard. They cleaned their belongings themselves, and the weekly sessions provided a chance for a chat and a gossip. Once their clothes and blankets were washed to their satisfaction, they hung them out to dry on the fence, and a wonderful array of patterns and colours shone in the morning light. There were geometrical designs and flowery ones, the latter large and blowsy and woven in startling pinks and reds on a black background.

"Ce faceți?" I showed my camera. "Aah, vreți o posă?" I wanted to take some photos of the bustling figures scrubbing their clothes with home-made soap on the round river stones beside the washing machine. There were five of them that morning, large and small, universally headscarved, they all wore the same flared kneelength skirts in black with gumboots on their feet and cardigans or jackets on top. They were all 'harnici', strong women, who looked as though they took life in their stride.

When I saw her again, I asked Georgeta about these weekly washing sessions.

"They are very important," she said. "It's a social occasion as well as a practical one. You know, during the communist period, the authorities closed down places where people came together to do business and could spend time talking to each other; they closed the mills for this reason. It was a way of making people obey them - if they couldn't exchange ideas there was less chance of dissent." The watermills and the washing whirlpools had been in decline; twenty years ago there were dozens of them, but now you could count the working ones on the fingers of two hands.

Looms with a View

Weaving is an important part of the Maramureș economy and many houses have their own looms. It is 'women's work', just as driving the horse and cart is a man's. It seems part of the natural order of things. Spinning and weaving are done during the winter months when the farm becomes less demanding, and since the Revolution, some of the weavers have turned their skills into a thriving cottage industry. Maramureș homespun has found its way into top fashion magazines. In 2000 *Egg* carried a feature on the chunky woollen slipers bordered with black velvet which have been made here since the Revolution. The material is the same as the stuff the weavers use for the thick woollen suits that men wear in winter.

On another trip I visited Mrs. Pipas, who used to make carpets for Communist Party officials. Her designs were so popular that she was able to build up a collection of antiques on the proceeds. Mrs. Pipas told me that making a carpet involved twenty separate processes. She used the traditional geometric patterns of chevrons and interlocking diamonds. All her dyes were natural. When I mentioned chemical dyes I sensed a hint of disapproval, as though using these would have been an affront to her religion. Her dyes included several types of onion skin and walnut. Walnut juice helped protect the wool against moths. She did not mention madder, but I had seen vats of the startling crimson liquid in other weavers' dyeing yards. It was used to colour the thick, shaggy, loose-weave blankets called 'cergi' that were once used to keep farm animals warm at night.

Mrs Pipas has a rival. Not long after the Revolution a priest's wife established a weavers' cooperative in the village of Botiza. It was one of the few occasions that I had heard the word used positively. Victoria Berbecăru had also researched the old patterns, and she encouraged a handful of local women to try them out. She helped them to buy wool and dyes, she obtained grants so they could adapt their homes for tourists. She also converted part of the parish house so that they could display the weavings and sell them. Some thirty households are involved in the project, and Botiza is confident in its new identity as a tourist and crafts centre. Today you can go to Botiza and learn the old skills of dyeing and weaving, and if crafts do not interest you, you can wander over the lovely hills instead.

The Hatter of Sârbi

Sârbi had woken up to tourism too: in its main street there was a new 'motel'. It was like no other motel I had seen. Fitted into the space of a small farmyard were a bar-cum-restaurant, an open air café, a trout hatchery and a spanking new fulling mill. The main part of the motel consisted of a two-storey concrete house, and the owner had furnished it with imitation Biedermeyer furniture from Germany. He was very proud of the furniture, although he was an able carpenter himself. I wanted to tell him how much nicer his own work was than the imported cupboards and dressers, but I was afraid of hurting his feelings. The restaurant-cum-bar was a brand new wooden chalet in the traditional style complete with 'prispa' (verandah). The open air café stood on a grove of trees and was covered by a pitched roof on tall, slender pillars; it had a couple of tables and benches made out of narrow wooden planks. The mill was a copy of the 19th century fulling mill which he had sold to the open air museum in Sibiu, in southern Transylvania. But the new one did not work as well.

Across the road lived a hatter called Ioan Bârlea. He worked in his sitting room at a heavy industrial sewing machine, and his wares - hats for men made of straw and woodchip - lay around him in neat piles. Ioan's twelve year old son sat with us while I watched him run up a clop in the blink of an eye. He used a long, single strand of straw which he had already plaited so that it was about half a centimetre wide and, starting with a twist at the centre of the crown, fed it through his fingers to the sewing machine, growing the shape as he went. As he sewed he talked; his kind face was creased with lines of sadness and worry. I learnt that his wife was in hospital and he could barely pay for her treatment. His son shifted closer to comfort his dad.

Ioan was using woodchip for some of his clopuri. I wondered why. He picked up a few slender strands of glossy, deep golden straw.

"I can't get enough of this any more," he said. "It's a special kind and nobody wants to spend the time growing it these days, let alone sorting and grading it; it takes too long. Woodchip is much cheaper and there's plenty around." Woodchip was a pale imitation of the straw. After the hat was stitched together it had to be damped and consolidated in a lead mould so that it would fit properly and not come apart. Ioan kept the clamp in his larder at the back of the house. For such a well-known craftsman he lived in very modest conditions. When I took my leave of them father and son stood by the gate, politely waving me goodbye. Then they turned and went back in the house, the man with his arm around the boy's shoulder.

...Şi hodina vântului mâi
Pă faţa pământului mâi dorule...

('...And the restfulness of the wind over the face of the Earth')

On that visit, I had all the time in the world. I climbed a short steep track to Biserica Susani, the Upper Church in Sârbi, and found it sheltering behind a row of ash, oak and hazel trees. A notice pinned to the door frame says it was built in 1532. The wood is bleached, but you can still see the carvings that decorate the door and windows. There are Slavonic crosses with three cross bars (the bottom one tilted), solar motifs and wolfs' tooth patterns. They are rough but attractive. The church stood in a corner of a large meadow where haystacks made black shadows in the afternoon sun. Further up the hill, beyond a tall hedge of willow and hazel, was a field full of dandelions. When the wind blew, millions of white clock heads surged this way and that like a foam-swept sea, sending clouds of seeds into the air. Further on up the hill the land became a mixture of rough scrub and pasture. There were few people around and, once again, the only sound I could hear apart from the rustling of individual leaves were the flute-like melodies of unseen birds, hammering, and barking dogs.

I lay down in the dry grass and looked back on the journey so far. Life was very tough here, and I knew I could not put up with such conditions for very long. But the richness and variety of traditions, the happy, cheerful way that people behaved, the astonishing beauty of the buildings and the landscape - these were all at risk if modernisation were to invade Maramureş. It was a constant, nagging theme: whether to save the best of what is there, or risk losing it for the sake of giving people 'civilised' living standards. The inadequacy of the terminology depressed me: what right had bureaucrats in remote city offices to decide how the country people should live? And by the same token, what right had I to tell them they should not have 'decent' homes? There was no denying that the greenness of the Maramureş, real and metaphorical, was good for my soul. But what about others? The Cosău Valley scheme was encouraging villagers to make the most of their homes and the installations like watermills and whirlpools by setting up bed-and-breakfast accommodation; it was also designed to help them sustain their traditional customs. I guessed that the revenue would not be great, but if it allowed them to live better while living as they were, surely that was a good thing?

Looking across to the opposite hillside with its traces of terracing, I could imagine settling down in this green haven, buying a cow and some geese, maybe a pig. When I walked down the hill towards the lower church, I met an old couple who were collecting hay.

"Don't you think we are primitive?" they joked, as though trying to hide some deep-seated shame.

"No, of course not," I said truthfully, "but how is life these days?"

"Cam grea", came the answer. Pretty hard.

Sârbi has a main street that goes on almost forever; towards one end where the tarmac peters out many of the wooden houses were decorated in a similar fashion to the church I had just seen: gates and porches were enlivened by sun symbols, trees of life, birds and rope motifs, their outlines worn soft by the years.

I had an introduction to a couple who were friends of friends. They did not refuse to help me, but there was an awkward moment while we decided if I could stay for a night and how much I should pay them for a bed. As soon as the deal had been struck the ţuica bottle came out. They told me they were used to putting up school children on exchange visits; they felt their house was not clean enough for me. Before nightfall, I helped to collect loose hay from the farmyard. They were filling their barn with the sweet-smelling grass ready for winter.

The next day I walked on to Budeşti. With around five thousand people, it is one of the largest villages. This is difficult to believe because the houses blend into the landscape. As in Sârbi, there are two parts to Budeşti, one upper and the other lower, and again, each has its timber church. Budeşti has a carpenter who makes monumental gates, a *vâltoare*, a public library and a school, and some of the women who live here weave their own carpets and clothes.

The Budeşti-Sârbi children's folk dance troupe uses the school for its practice sessions. They were going through their paces as I passed. The noise was like a hundred elephants doing the hokey-kokey in clogs: deafening and irresistible. Following the sound, I pushed a door open and found myself in a room with a concrete floor and a single window. It was grim: a bare, cold space, with a single electric light bulb. There were a lot of windows, but it was like a prison cell. Except for the children. There were around thirty boys and girls of between eight and twelve years old. They were wearing their ordinary clothes - leggings, nylon tooks, sweatshirts and trainers. Some of their gear, bearing well-known western logos, probably came from aid lorries or the second-hand shops which had sprouted up all over Romania since the Revolution. The colours made a splash in the spartan room. The children were lined up in crocodile formation, stamping and chanting as they moved forwards. At their head walked a tall, skeletal young man who was bending and weaving in time to a passionate 'învertita' that he was playing on his fiddle.

When they broke for a rest, the children clustered around me, demanding to know who I was, where I came from, what I was doing in Budeşti.

"Do you speek Eenglish?" some of them giggled, while others grabbed my hand and tried to pull me into the chorus line. The folk troupe from Budeşti-Sârbi has performed several times. It went to Paris in support of the Romanian World Cup team. It is one of the good things that came out of The Song to Romania.

Budeşti's lower church is known as Biserica Nemeşilor (the Nobles' Church) and it is a jewel of its kind. There are ropework carvings on gate pillars that are the size of an elephant's legs. The whole construction was solid and well-proportioned. The same held true for the interior. It had minute window openings, about six inches tall. They were pointed at the top, creating one of the simplest Gothic designs I had ever seen. The glass was thick and irregular; it had been hand-made. In the cemetery behind the church, where lichen-covered fruit trees bowed gnarled heads that were laden with bright red apples and russet coloured pears, was a row of about six wide flat stone slabs lying on the ground. It was a 'Masa Moşilor', the place where the village elders were fêted once a year with a feast of local delicacies and good cheer.

Budeşti's lower church had been built in 1643. By the 1990s the leaking roof had allowed the fabric to rot so badly that it has had to be completely reconstructed. Its stone foundations were renewed as well. When I first saw the church in 1995, the work had not started. Two years later, I watched local carpenters shape the heavy logs with hand tools, intent on their work and sure of what they were doing.

Three tourists in Maramureş

In 2001 Kit and I decided to go hiking in the Maramureş. Kit is my "partenerul de viaţa", my life partner and car mechanic. We invited a friend of ours called Sylvia to come with us. Sylvia is an American artist who has moved to the Orkney Islands. She showed her mettle early on in our journey by giving Kit and me nicknames which she used whenever we started bickering.

We took it in turns to drive. I was at the wheel when we drove into Prague late one evening and lost our way. With night-marish suddenness, I found myself racing along a tramline in the dark, with one front and back wheel up on the pavement.

"I said turn left back there."

"I didn't hear you, speak up!"

"What do you want me to do, write it down for you every time?"

"I don't know where we're going! For Christ's sake, there's a tram coming..."

"Now Fluffy, now Kerfuffle, take it easy. Just calm down, there's a lay-by right ahead..."

Sylvia frightened us by driving very fast along unknown roads with her head turned towards whoever was sitting beside her. The fact that she was talking brilliantly about art, manners and philosophy made it impossible to ask her to stop.

There was a path over the mountains from Budeşti to Poienile Izei. Some of the passes in this area had not been used since the Second World War. The best way to see them was to hire a horse and cart with a driver who knew the way. We asked Georgeta Iuga to act as our guide.

Georgeta was a brilliant guide, the kind who can impart accurate information in a way that makes it fun. But her determination and efficiency had something Germanic about it. She told me by

way of explanation that she had grown up on the south-eastern Transylvanian plateau near Sighișoara. This is the heart of Saxon Transylvania, colonised by German-speaking peoples since the 12th and 13th centuries. Their unshakeable self-reliance made itself felt in economic, cultural and political terms, and their passing, now that so many have left to find a better life in the Fatherland, is much regretted. Transylvanians still regard themselves as a cut above the rest because of the Germans' orderliness.

The five of us set out on a dazzling morning and swung south-east out of Budeşti. We took a stony road beside a tumbling stream and climbed up into the hills. Detritus from the winter floods was strewn on either side of the brook. A few weeks ago the track had been submerged. Beside it, the houses gradually thinned out, like beads on a much-repaired necklace. In their place came close-cropped meadows and the scrubby pastures of the open hill-sides. Long tufts of last year's pale, dead grass covered the ground. Once or twice, a 'Roman' lorry would thunder past us on its way to or from a quarry. After an hour we passed the limits of their capabilities and peace reigned. Then the stone track disappeared too and we struck out across the clumps of springy grass. It had been a hard winter. We followed intermittent parallel ruts and sheep runs, looking back every so often to admire the view which fell away behind us in an ever more magnificent panorama. This was the high, open pasture where people came to cut isolated crops of hay or graze their flocks. There were few trees. The sky was huge.

Half way to the top we came to an Orthodox monastery. It was in the process of being built. There were only two buildings, the timber church and the administrative offices. Wooden scaffolding and tubs of paint and plaster stood around. The priest and a handful of nuns and local people were there too, with their sleeves rolled up.

"Salut, salut, buna ziua; ce mai faceți; Dumnezeu vă ajuta; săru' mână..." We exchanged the proper greetings, shaking hands or having them kissed in the old-fashioned way. The priest was Fratele Ioan, who had once flown commercial aircraft for Tarom, Romania's national airline. He was still young and was teaching himself English by reading Dickens. Brother Ioan invited us to a lunch of potato soup, fresh white bread and spring water from the mountain. They could not have tasted better if they had been foie gras, asparagus and Chablis.

When we left the monastery, two women started up the mountain side with us. They had spent the morning helping in the church. Rubbernecking and taking photographs, we were too slow for them and after ten minutes they veered away from us, and marched off along a shortcut to the mountain pass in their 'opinci' (home-made, boat-shaped leather shoes tied with thongs), their calf-length skirts swinging in unison. We stopped on the broad ridge to rest the horses and let them graze; then their driver turned them home again: we would have to carry our bags from here. Minuscule yellow and purple orchids were flowering among the herbs, the plantains and the prickly grasses. I saw pinks the size of a small finger nail and cobalt gentians, past their best but still startling. They mirrored the sky. Small spruce trees dotted the hill top in clusters. The air smelt good.

Poienile Izei was a cluster of houses in the valley below us. Georgeta pointed out Glod and Botiza in the distance. Getting to our destination meant slipping and hopping down the mountain beside a watercourse. Like monkeys, we swung ourselves down to the branches of overhanging beech trees and hazel shrubs with leaves as large as pingpong bats. The breeze smelt of nuts and mulch.

On the lower slopes we met the two women from the monastery again. We greeted each other like old friends. Civilisation began when the faltering meadow track became a hoof-printed footpath with high banks on either side. As we passed a tall, wooden barn in a small-holding to our left, its doors sprang open and two bay horses leapt out at a gallop, pulling a cart behind them. In the driving seat was an old man, bent over like a jockey with the effort of controlling his steeds. A woman slammed the doors shut again and ran after him. Equipage and driver rattled and bounced past us; Georgeta called to the woman and the snorting horses were pulled up. They carried our luggage for us, depositing it a mile ahead with Marioara, our landlady, so that we could saunter into Poienile Izei as though we had been on a Sunday stroll.

I knew the village from Kosei Miya's photographs. The Japanese photographer had come to Romania in 1968 when he was still a student. He fell in love with the Maramureş and kept returning. I do not know anyone who has captured the confidence and simplicity of its people better than him.

The wooden church in Poienile Izei is no longer used except for special occasions. It is overshadowed by a much larger, concrete church, but holds its own for sheer beauty of line. Inside, witty scenes from the Last Judgment frescoes warn parishioners against the evils of laziness and usury.

We stayed in a neat, modern house at the other end of the village. Our landlady was Marioara. She made us a slap-up supper of sausages, mashed potato and pickles followed by home-made cakes. We chased the food down with bottles of Silva beer. While we were finishing our meal, two neighbours arrived to meet us, and soon the table cloth disappeared under a rag-taggle army of brown bottles.

Georgeta worked as an archaeologist and anthropologist. She supplemented a meagre income at Baia Mare's village museum by painting traditional icons and glass and making bead necklaces. She was married to a poet called Dumitru who could trace his ancestry back to the time of Bogdan of Cuhea, the 14th century founder of independent Moldavia, when his forebears owned a neighbouring estate. In a sense this made them 'nemeşi'. The hardships of life under communism and a rock-solid faith in Christian morals convinced the Iugas that after the Revolution they should devote their lives to the preservation of Maramureş's unique customs and beliefs. It had not been an easy decision. Two years before the Ceauşescus met their nemesis, the couple were in England visiting friends, something most Romanians at the time could only dream of. It made me wonder if they had been Party members to enjoy such privileges. But I did not ask; the Iugas had their own dreams which made their position crystal clear. Over coffee, I asked Georgeta to explain what had happened to them in those heady days, nearly a decade ago.

"We could have stayed in England, but Dumitru wanted to come back because he said 'our fight is in Romania'. After 1990 we did not even think of leaving the country; we wanted to build a better society here. If somebody had asked us to die for Romania, we would have done it with pleasure, for the good of the country. It's pathetic, I know! When the Revolution started we were out celebrating in the streets of Baia Mare and we were happy. Dumitru printed the first edition of a free newspaper called 'Maiastră' (a mythical bird in Romanian folklore, and the name of a sculpture by Brân-cuşi). He sent me home, saying that if one of us was killed the other should be safe to look after the children. On 1 January 1990 every-body had a copy of Maiastră. I think it cost 1 leu (soon afterwards the leu was devalued and there are currently about 45,000 lei to the British pound). Then Dumitru printed another edition giving the names of some Securitate agents. That's when our dreams started to collapse. We received death threats and Dumitru was shot at. There was a smear campaign against us. I couldn't stand it, so I started painting icons; they gave me an escape." Georgeta's voice was steady, but her hands were shaking.

The next day, we hired another cart and walked over a pass from Sârbi back to Budeşti. Lost on a mountain track that was hid-den under dead leaves, we heard a voice ring out from the stygian depths of the encroaching fir trees:

"Cine sunteţi?"

A man followed the voice. He was dressed in loden hunting clothes and a hat with a feather in it. A rifle was slung over his shoulder. He was a forester, paid by Romsilva, Romania's state-owned forestry commission, to make sure no one stole or damaged the trees. His job seemed redundant; from what we could see and hear, Second World War partisans could easily have been the last people to show any interest in the woodland round about us. A vel-vety silence had closed in again. As though to confirm our impres-

sion, the forester was very laid back and invited us to mid-day drinks in his cabin. Then he hitched a ride on our cart.

We trundled on, following his directions until the track plunged down a gulley and we came up short against a traffic jam. A huge tree trunk was blocking the way; attached to it at the other end by chains was a pair of exhausted horses who were covered in sweat. We all took a hand and eventually shifted the trunk so that our cart could squeeze past. The forester seemed unperturbed; they would sort it out. We left the trees and crossed a grassy ridge; over the brow in the middle of a wide sward of rough grass was a log cabin. A verandah ran along its front and the door was open. As we drew level with the door, three men came out of it. They were wearing the same kind of forester's uniform, minus the hat. With Georgeta translating for us, they made us feel as welcome as long lost relations. We probably broke the monotony of a very boring job. Soon the țuica and beer were flowing. Kit was smiling pleasantly but I knew he was baulking inside: he had had seven glasses of țuica already that morning. It was easier for Sylvia and me to refuse the brandy; no-one expected women to take it as a matter of course. For a man, it was different. We knew that once the țuica had been poured it was regarded as a sign of bad luck to leave any behind. Between the nine of us, we made a sizeable dent in the two-litre bottle.

That day we lunched in the open. We were on the broad, soft top of the mountain pass looking towards the thousand metre peak of Chicera. There were plenty of accommodating hollows made for

picnics but it was chilly up there. Under Georgeta's directions we gathered dry, dead wood and pulled it together in a circle. Then she rubbed two dry sticks together and put the spark to a small pile of desiccated grass. Half an hour later we were warming our hands at a terrific blaze. Chewing fresh bread, crisp slices of fire-grilled slanina (pig fat with the skin left on) and ceapa (onion), I realised an extraordinary thing: there was no litter anywhere, not even a flattened ring pull from a coke can. If this idyllic landscape were tidied up and made safe for hikers and tourists, its natural beauty would be compromised. Suddenly I wished the human race would just go away. As we made our way down to Budeşti, the weather broke. The sky turned dark violet and forks of lightning crackled over our heads. Sylvia was sitting in the cart behind the driver while Kit and I stumbled along behind trying not to fall to our knees. At that point the track went sharply downhill and for a few seconds I lost sight of her. When I reached the same point, I saw her below me, clinging desperately to the sides as the vehicle pitched and twisted down a streaming gulley. The driver had hopped out to wind on the back brake, and then rushed to his horses' heads to keep them steady. Huddled in her macintosh cloak and broad-brimmed leather hat as the rain slashed down, Sylvia looked like a Wild West pioneer.

In the distance slender spirals of woodsmoke rose from unseen chimneys in the forests close to the village, and there was light in the sky. A mile or so out from Budeşti we joined a real wagon train. Three or four carts were ahead of us; some farmers were coming home from market. As the downpour subsided we waved at them and got sympathetic grins in response. The couple in front of us had a yearling colt with them. They were letting him run free, trusting that he would follow his dam, one of the pair that was pulling their cart. The colt was black, proud and beautiful, and pranced beside us on long, clean legs with a zest and cheekiness that I hoped would not be beaten out of him too soon. As our horses plodded wearily homewards, he bounded about, sampling a patch of herbs here and dawdling there, then galloping away over the endless pasture with head and tail high before returning to cajole and tease and start the exuberant cycle all over again.

In upper Budeşti there was a wooden house for sale. If I did not buy it, the chances were it would be torn down and burnt for firewood. It had a shingled roof, a verandah with arching branches on either side of the sturdy posts and two tiny rooms each one with a box bed. It would have only cost £200, but I did not have the funds, and there was another problem: I would have had to find somewhere to put it. At the time foreigners could not buy land in Romania unless they registered a company there. Reluctantly we left the house to its fate.

Georgeta ran a charity that helped families keep their children at school. On the way back down to our B & B, she asked us to go with her to visit a woman who had problems of this kind. The house was a humble wooden cottage on the edge of the village. When Georgeta knocked at the door, the woman was busy weaving textiles with her sister. Although we were interrupting her, she invited us in and offered us coffee as though the meeting had been fixed in her diary for weeks. Her name was Anca. The loom was a gigantic contraption that filled the entire front room, leaving just enough space for a huge black and white TV set. We sidled in through the door and sat down to watch the two women at work in the semi-dark. They were tying strings to shuttles, making sure each one was the required length, before starting a carpet. Sylvia and I took photographs of them and their handiwork. I still have the slides. In them the sisters are nearly identical, with round faces, olive skins, pink cheeks and strong eyebrows. Their glossy black hair is tied back with clips. They look the picture of rude health. Both sisters were married and they had eleven children between them. Their husbands were layabouts who spent their money on drink. When they got drunk they beat up their wives. Georgeta wanted to help Anca's twelve year old son who was clever. From their conversation she learnt that he was more interested in smoking with older boys than staying in school. She told his mother there would be no cash unless he completed the year. At supper Georgeta explained that her charity only gave grants to children whose parents would support them and who genuinely wanted to succeed. She provided half their expenses for a year at school, and sometimes contributed towards college fees; the parents had to come up with the rest. When we talked about Anca's son, the corners of Georgeta's mouth turned down. She said it was probably too late to save him. I had never seen her thwarted before; in such a strong character it was a shock.

Poverty in the countryside never seems as bad as it does in towns. Budeşti is a thriving village as villages go: there are people making some kind of living by carpentry, making straw hats and selling their milk and cheese. There are lots of children and the school provides a focal point for the community. We watched men mending shingled roofs, generously overlapping the split pine tiles to prevent leaks. Sometimes the carpentry was crude, but it was the proportions that held the eye. It would have been easy to eulogise the life of Budeşti, but I wondered how closely knit the people were. There was lots of activity in the streets, and if life here was not idyllic then it was not dead either. As tourists, we were seeing it through rose-coloured lenses. With Georgeta we had an anthropologist on hand, so I asked her whether Budeşti had a community spirit.

"Extended families help each other - they call it the 'claca'," Georgeta told us, "but help between neighbours is not so common."

Along the main street which passed the Lower Church the road was lined on either side with monumental wooden gates. As expressions of individuality, pride and self-respect they were creaking perilously close to collapse. Wood was giving way to brick and plastic; every other house had its satellite dish. The question which still nagged me was whether or not the picturesque customs and skills had a chance of survival. I wanted to help my friends here by bringing small groups of walkers out from the UK. But would any form of tourism, no matter how sensitive, spell the end for what I loved about Maramureş? With relief I recalled Gail Kligman's opinion from 'The Wedding of the Dead', the book that she wrote about Ieud in the mid-1980s. Some things would surely vanish, she admitted, but the Maramureşeani have a way of absorbing change without losing their identity. To illustrate her point, Gail Kligman focussed on their attitude to death. The burial rites which they have evolved allow people to grieve with abandon, to encompass their pain and move on. There has been change in the musical traditions already. Derby-born Lucy Castle plays with Ioan Pop in the band Popeluc. She has learnt to play Maramureş fiddle tunes like a native and she studied the repertoire for her doctorate. We met her at Tânjaua that year. Lucy has noticed that local bands are introducing contemporary western idioms. "They aren't copying them slavishly but playing them in a distinctly Maramureş style. I've got a feeling they may create something totally new." Change is natural; 'adapt or die'. My vision of an eternally green, eternally contented land of wooden houses and horse-drawn carts was surely doomed.

Georgeta had a house in Şurdeşti, a village that lies to the south of Cavnic. She had built it with her own money, hoping to use it as a base for ethnographic workshops and field trips. It was also a holiday cottage and she invited us to stay. The house was a pint-sized chalet made of pine logs. They were still pale yellow and new-looking. A small verandah led into a large kitchen-cum-sitting and dining room, and there were two bedrooms upstairs in the roof space. It stood in the middle of a hay orchard set far back from the road and you could only reach it on foot.

Şurdeşti boasts the tallest wooden spire in Europe; it sits atop a timber church, looking impressive but top heavy. Church and spire have been restored, but the thirty-four metre tower has lost the record: the nuns of nearby Bârsana built a taller one in 1998. Inside the paintings are from the late 18th and early 19th century, expressions of a Westernised Byzantine folk art as peculiar as they are fetching. The churchyard is fringed with walnut and mulberry trees, and there are antique grave stones in a cemetery shaded by damson and pear.

To the west of Şurdeşti village there is an outcrop of rocks about two hundred feet high. They tower over the orchards, and someone has planted a Romanian flag at the top. There is some graffiti too. It says that Romania has the best football team in the world. Other people have made their mark here. At the foot of the cliff face there is a rock cube, eight feet high and shrouded by ash trees. On its flat crown there are signs of a runic script, scarcely visible, and the burn marks of a prehistoric fire. If you stand up you can see far into the distance down along successive valleys. If you shouted from here, your voice would carry for miles. In ivy-covered caves formed by the rubble we found faint Christian crosses, visible if you held a lighted match to one side. No-one has studied them seriously and we could only speculate on why they were there. Thracians and members of related tribes held out in the Carpathians until the 10th century; maybe these rocks had been a safe haven for them and their ancestors.

Historical Pastoral

In 1995, President Iliescu said that Romanians were Dacs who came from the Tracs (he pronounced the words in English as 'ducks' and 'trucks'). The claim was full of poetic licence. Like most of us, Romanians are liquorice allsorts, but his statement contained some truth. The Thracians were great pastoralists and speculating on the legacy of their sheep culture adds immeasurably to the pleasure of visiting a fold or 'stână' (stuhna). Many Romanian villages have a collective system of animal care which has nothing to do with the communist period. Sheep, cattle, goats and geese from all the households are looked after by dedicated herdsmen who go out day after day, to graze the animals on common land belonging to the village. Shepherds are a cut above the rest, having their own mythology, customs and accoutrements. One of Romania's best known legends is the Miorița, a story about a young shepherd who allows two other shepherds to kill him without trying to escape. Miorița is supposedly a Dacian myth, although it is not exclusive to Romania. Scholars say it is an allegory for a proto-Christian faith and that the Dacians learnt their philosophical disinterestedness from the Pythagoreans. Romanians say, only half joking, that that is why they are so good at turning the other cheek.

On our second day in Şurdeşti we hired Georgeta's neighbour Vasile and his superb bay horse for a trip to a stână. A heap of hay wrapped in tarpaulin provided us with a comfy seat and the horse with some spare lunch. Several cergi, fresh white loaves, fruit and coffee were stacked in the back of the cart as well. We set off at a spanking pace up the hill to Cavnic. The morning was misty and, as we left the road, we could only see a few yards in front of our faces. It was cold in the cart so we got out and walked. Vasile led us up through groves of fruit trees and along grassy tracks that petered out into meadowland. The ground was full of interesting mounds and hollows that could have been made by humans. We walked over springy clumps of aromatic lemon thyme, and skirted spinneys of beech and hazel. We were alone except for one or two solitary cow-herds who were whittling sticks to while away the time, or sleeping on the grass. Their cattle were handsome, fat red creatures that chewed the cud in lazy disdain. The air was heavy with potential rain and, after a pregnant pause, it started to drizzle.

The rain stopped soon afterwards and miraculously the sun came out. At last we could gaze out over the green mountains around us. Imagination provided what the eye could not: hope that their beauty would last. Nobody felt like speaking; it was the ideal moment for some sweet melancholia. As we came over the brow of the next hill, the stână appeared and my mood evaporated. All it was was a corral and a shack. The corral was made of willow hurdles and the shack consisted of three rusting sheets of iron held up at the front and sides with branches. There was a fire in the opening and a big black cauldron standing to one side. There were four men in the corral with a milling flock of a couple of hundred sheep.

Vasile hurriedly uncoupled his horse from the cart, hobbled him with a chain, threw a cergă over his back and rushed over to the corral. It was his turn to help with the milking. The sheep have to be milked three times a day and the shepherds take it in turns to do this, and to stay with the flocks overnight to keep the animals safe from wolves, bears and thieves. The days of the great treks, when shepherds would take their sheep on foot across hundreds of miles to and from their summer pastures, have not entirely died out in Romania, but Şurdeşti had no need of such epic transhumance. Enormous flocks, containing thousands of animals, were a thing of the past. They had grown to these sizes during the medieval period when the Saxons introduced weaving technology to Transylvania, and afterwards when parts of Romania came under Turkish rule. Although not in such vast numbers, sheep had continued to make money for Transylvanian shepherds under the communists. That was the rumour in any case. Curious to see whether or not there was truth in the story, I had been to some of the villages in southern Transylvania where these wealthy shepherds were reputed to live. Behind the massive, forbidding gates of village farms I had caught glimpses of shining 4x4s, while on the hillsides around Sibiu men rode donkeys to round up their flocks. They made striking figures in their long, sheepskin cloaks that reached from neck to ankle. If these were the rich countrymen I had heard about, they kept their loot well hidden.

When it came to milking, the shepherds at this stâna worked as a team. First, the sheep were driven from the pasture into a small outer corral. Then each man sat on a stool next to a hole in the fencing, grabbed one of the sheep, milked it and shoved it head first through the hole. After a few days they move the corral several yards away so that the ground does not get too sour.

It is always relaxing to watch other people work. While Vasile busied himself with the milking we took shelter from the drizzle which had started again and warmed our soggy feet by the fire. Georgeta tore up some bread and opened a bottle of ţuica. The dreaded liquid came into its own as a general pick-me-up and blood circulator.

As the feeling came back into my toes I had a look at my surroundings. For a simple shelter, it was amazingly well-appointed. Three piles of blankets laid on the ground showed where the shepherds slept. In the corners they had stacked essential equipment: hand-made wooden bowls, cups and tubs; enamelled saucepans; perforated metal spoons for ladelling curds; an axe and a saw for cutting firewood; a polished wooden saddle decorated with incised dots and crosses. Having only seen such objects in museums before, I stared in disbelief. The saddle had been shaped with a pommel and cantle but it looked as comfortable as a form of medieval torture. Stacked in another corner was a bundle of shepherds' crooks. One of them drew my eyes like a magnet; it was a lovely piece of work, with a goat's head at the top and carvings all the way down. I pulled myself up and brought it out into the light where I could examine it more easilly. Then I nearly dropped the crook: the carvings were sexual fantasies featuring a well-developed male figure. They spiralled along the shaft like engravings on a miniature Trajan's Column.

"What's that?" asked Kit, seeing me go pink.

"Nothing... just some drawings."

Sylvia cocked an eyebrow.

"Let's have a look." She put on her reading specs and came closer. "... Aah, I see," she grinned at me, an unshockable Virginian who was once a resident artist on a sheep farm in the Scottish borders. "I guess they get lonely up here."

Once the milk was collected, the shepherds turned it into a soft cheese called 'brânza'. They boiled the liquid in the cauldron, adding a commercial coagulating agent, then separated the curds and whey. They drained the curds in calico cloths and hung them from nails on a makeshift four-legged shelf that stood beside the shelter. When it had set, the cheese was sweet and delicious. Vasile kept offering us more of it. With no fridge it was the only way they could use the milk. The dormant entrepreneur in me woke up: surely this was an organic food salesman's dream: think of the advertising! Mountain-pure milk with no (well, hardly any!) additives. Some of the cheese was sold locally, but after sating ourselves on it, there was masses left over. Vasile admitted they got sick of it, day after day.

The shepherds took turns to stay overnight at the fold. There is a custom which dictates that the fire must be kept going throughout the spring; to let it go out spells bad luck. For us it had been a blessing. Even in May the temperature was much colder up there than in the valley below.

Every May in the hills above villages in Maramureş and nearby Oaş people take a day off for the annual milk measuring ceremony. In Romanian the custom is called 'Ruptul sterpelor', and Maramureş is one of the few places where it is still celebrated. Sterp means barren and ruptul sterpelor refers to the separation of the sheep or cows which are in milk from those that are barren. The shepherds give the owners an amount milk in proportion to the number of animals they own. Although it functions as an annual audit, the custom is also an excuse for a party. As soon as the measuring is finished, blankets and cloths are spread out over the meadow and out come the horinca, the bread, the strips of bacon fat, the pickles and the cakes. Often a lamb is sacrificed to the feast as well.

Carpathian sheepdogs are nothing like British border collies. Instead they are shaggy bruisers that are bred to fight with wolves. Vasile and his friends had a pack of them. They remained wary of us at the stâna, and threw themselves down on the other side of the corral. To protect them, the dogs wear metal collars studded with spikes.

Three hours passed by in the shake of a lamb's tail. Vasile stayed behind to take his shift, so we walked back down to Şurdeşti, happy with our day out and eager for many more.

The House on the Corner

Vasile's wife Maria looked after Georgeta's house. Her nickname was Maria din Colţ, Maria from the Corner, because she lived on a corner of the valley road between Baia Mare and Cavnic. Maria's house was divided into two parts, one dark and spartan for everyday use, the other clean and spruce for special occasions. The house for

special use was furnished with long net curtains, heavily ornamented pelmets and soft rugs, some garish, nylon and factory-made
and others woven in wool. Maria was immensely proud of her clean
house, and I felt it was a privilege to be shown inside. She would
not let me into the other part of the house because she was ashamed
of its modesty. Opposite was a huge wooden barn, and on the
fourth side of her estate was a combined pig sty and cart shed. The
whole farmstead was only twenty yards across from end to end.
Maria must have had some furrows of land somewhere, but her
home seemed peripheral to the general landscape, as if she was a
squatter there, not its lady and mistress.

Maria din Colţ was terribly anxious. Once or twice she gave
way to tears. As we were about to leave, she broke down again, and
at last we found out why. Her two sons were working illegally
abroad. She had not heard from them in weeks and she could not
reach them by telephone. Desperate, she threw herself on me and
begged me to help her. It was an ironic scenario: at home the UK
government was making political capital out of 'economic refugees'
and how to get rid of them. A lot of our righteous indignation was
aimed at Romanians, and more often, Romanian Gypsies. And here
was Maria sick with worry about her boys. All I could do was offer
some sympathy. It did not seem nearly enough. Vasile was less de-
monstrative; it was hard to say how this situation affected him. He
reacted to most eventualities with a sardonic smile.

Old ground and new

The following autumn I drove to Romania again, this time on my
own. Back in the Maramureş I felt as though I had never been away.
I called on Maria one afternoon while I was driving past. As soon as
I saw her it was clear that things had improved: her face was glowing. Without preamble she told me her sons were OK, she had a
mobile number and they were getting legal work permits.

I went to Bogdan Vodă, formerly Cuhea. It had changed its
name in memory of Prince Bogdan of Moldavia who came from
here. Bogdan was not the first Maramureşean to explore the other
side of the Carpathians: earlier in the 14th century his countrymen
had fought for the Hungarian king in Moldavia when the Magyars'
eastern frontier guards, the Székely borderers, came under attack
from Crimean Tartars. It was not as complicated as it sounds. Moldavia was a corridor between the Carpathians and the Black Sea; its
fertile land was segmented into pockets which were dominated by
Catholic, Orthodox and animist peoples, both settlers and nomads.
Over the past thousand years, with no geographical barriers to protect it from the north, it had been subject to invasions from Central

Asia and Scandinavia, and from the Turkic, Iranian and Arab territories of the Near and Middle East. In the end it was the men from Maramureş who conquered medieval Moldavia. First came the legendary Dragoş who claimed a small part of the country after a hunting expedition, then a few princes who ruled a wider area in Hungary's name, and finally Bogdan from Cuhea, in defiance of the Magyar autocracy.

Bogdan was a founder of the Moldavian Muşat dynasty and his successors built extraordinary churches, palaces and fortresses. Bogdan's native village is less exciting. Its main street goes on for mile after dusty mile. It has charm though. In the village centre, there is a gorgeous wooden church right by the road. Its only drawback is that the modern church next door dwarfs it completely. Inside there are paintings showing scenes from the medieval wars with the Ottomans. Outside, a wooden belt, or 'brâu', carved to look like a thick cord, runs right around it. Like the one at Deseşti, it symbolises the infinity of God's love. But it is completely overshadowed by a grand new edifice of brick and concrete, Bogdan Voda's modern Orthodox church, and now, nearly three hundred years after being built, it has become redundant. Further along the road I found the shed which houses the ruins of the oldest stone church in Maramureş. It was built in the 12th century. All that is left are the foundations, but they mean a lot to local Romanian historians. For reasons of religious intolerance, the Hungarian kings forbade the Maramureşeani to build their churches in stone.

Un-de ud   cu - cu cân - tând -, Un-de aud   cu -cu

cân - tând -, Merg în cod - ru tăt plang - ând - -,

Merg în cod-ru   tăt plan gând le hai şi hai mâi dor-u - le - -.

('When I hear the cuckoo calling I go to the forest weeping...')

To the north of Bogdan Vodă there is a fork in the road. Follow it to the south and you arrive in Ieud. For two years during the 1980s the American ethnographer Gail Kligman had lived here. She had already written her doctoral thesis on a banned Romanian custom that celebrated the coming of spring called Căluş. What she found here became the subject of her second book, The Wedding of the Dead. Ieud was one of the villages which the communists left alone, realising that collectivisation would not work there. Ieudeni resisted collectivisation and maintained their folk rituals. It was the women who kept these traditions alive, and it was they who put up the most stubborn, if passive, resistance.

The Wedding of the Dead was once known over much of medieval Europe, but the practice had apparently only survived here in Maramureş and maybe in some other Balkan countries. If a child or a young person died before they were married, their neighbours would arrange a symbolic wedding to ensure them a safe passage into the next world. If the young person was male, he would be accompanied to his grave by a sapling decorated with ribbons and flowers, to symbolise his 'wife'. If it was a girl, she would be ritually married to Christ before being interred. I never heard of cremations in Maramureş villages. The Wedding of the Dead was still practised in Ieud. Every stage of the ritual was accompanied by special verses, sung by women and handed down by them to the next generation.

Ieud is one of those villages that practises endogamy. It was not easy to win the people's trust, although as a foreigner Gail Kligman presented less of a threat than if she had come from nearby Şieu. She faithfully recorded the long chants which accompany the symbolic weddings of young people who die before their time. I could imagine the half shouted, half sobbing cry, having already heard it in Deseşti. Such singing was a physical way of taking the edge off grief. It was a ritual that allowed hope for continuity.

If any church deserves the title of cathedral, Ieud's magnificent Biserica în Vale (The Church in the Vale) is surely one of them. It has a colossal roof with a ridge so sharp that it cuts the sky like a blade. The building is stained a rich, dark chestnut brown that glows in the sunlight. Its doors and window openings are decorated with enough carvings to look rich but not fussy. It used to have a superb collection of glass icons which dated as far back as its foundation in 1717. Since the Revolution they had started to go missing, and the remainder were put safely under lock and key in a museum somewhere. The empty spaces had been filled with modern copies.

Sitting under the eaves in their dashing Sunday best, about thirty women were listening to readings from the Bible. It was their clothes that caught my eye. Traditional dress in the Maramureş consists of two woollen aprons, one at the back and one at the front, worn over a white underskirt with a white, embroidered blouse and waistcoat on top and black, calf-length leather boots below. The aprons have wide horizontal stripes consisting of one plain colour, usually black, alternating with another which is often bright red, but sometimes orange or yellow, or a combination of hues including green, black and blue. More often than not, the wool is coloured with vivid chemical dyes, and the effect is astonishing.

Listening reverently to Bible readings in the afternoon sun, the women of Ieud looked like a row of exotic bees taking an unaccustomed rest. Children rushed in and out of the churchyard, but they did not disturb the reading. Used to the tension of city life, I expected a parental explosion, but none came. Nobody hushed the laughing, playing children or even frowned at them. There was no need. The church was more like an extension of their own homes than a place where they went as a duty or to make a show of piety once a week. They looked after the church and in return it embraced them.

There was another wooden church in the village. It was older than this one by 350 years. Crossing the Ieud stream, I made the short, stiff climb up the hill to Biserica din Deal (the Church on the Hill). It was worth the effort. Much smaller than its Greco-Catholic cousin in the valley below, this pocket-sized Orthodox shrine had been constructed in 1364. It was a rare survivor in this land where perishable wood buildings were lucky to last more than two hundred years. I found the key-keeper and asked her to open the door for me. Inside, everything was dark. The ceiling in the pronaos was very low and the atmosphere smelt pungently of incense, candle-smoke, damp and human bodies. Tucked into one side of the room there was a staircase made from a single oak trunk. It went up into the gallery. This was the church where Zbornicul de la Ieud, that 14th century book of laws, had been found. Zbornicul contained three manuscripts written in Romanian but transcribed with Cyrillic characters. They were the earliest examples of Romanian writing ever recorded. When they were translated the texts turned out to be cooking recipes.

Holding a torch to the walls I could just make out the outlines of frescos. They were damaged by rain and candle smoke, but I could see that they were done in the same simple, graphic style as the paintings I had seen elsewhere in Maramureş. The pictures turned out to be by Alexandru Ponehalski, one of the best known religious artists in the Maramureş. He made these paintings in 1782.

The building was sturdy as well as beautiful. Subtle details added to its charm: the curved pine logs in the walls on the north and south sides were graded so that they became gradually smaller all the way up. The ceiling of the naos was in the shape of a polyhedron instead of a plain barrel vault, and the candelabra were made of wood.

Ieud keeps its secrets well. Much later I discovered that there was an old Jewish cemetery above the village. It was a reminder of

Part II

Moldavia

Moldavia is roughly four times larger than Maramureș. Touching Ukraine in the north, it reaches from the Carpathians in the west to the Prut River in the east, and travels as far south as the Bărăgan Plain. The country encompasses alpine pastures enfolded in giant spruce forests, as well as steppe and rolling, black-soiled agricultural land that is patterned with strips of grain, maize and root vegetables.

Clods and sods: down to earth in old Moldavia

I was travelling on horseback with a group of English people and two Romanian mountain hunters (soldiers from the mounted division at Mircurea Ciuc). We were on a six-week expedition to follow the campaign trail of the 15th century Moldavian prince, Stephen the Great. Stephen stood out from all the other Moldavian princes for his qualities as a leader, his cultivated mind, his buildings, and for his expertise in guerilla warfare. He withstood a Turkish invasion without any help from the richer countries of western Europe, and won more than thirty battles. Pope Sixtus III called him an Athlete of Christ.

Although the expedition was a unique opportunity, logistically it was impossible. Before long, some of the English turned it into a farce of squabbling and jealousy. I was soon at loggerheads with the organisers, but we learnt something, even if it was not what we expected. While the riders fought over management problems, the soldiers sloped along with us, detached from our quarrels, and enjoying their paid holiday and the chance to catch up on some sleep. Later we had an escort of military police (we must have been a suspicious-looking lot) and the MPs brought a television along with them. They watched it every night in the back of their lorry.

The contrast between what we were doing and the life of people around us was painfully sharp, and it became sharper the further east across Moldavia we went. In the foothills to the west of Rădăuți, a couple of young men were laboriously earthing up rows of beetle-infested potatoes with a horse-drawn plough. On the outskirts of Suceava, a worried householder asked me not to let my pony eat the grass outside her fence. She had been keeping it for her chickens. Down in the nondescript plains between Vaslui and Iași, a man and two young boys rushed at us angrily with pitchforks because we were riding through a hay crop. We were trying to avoid the traffic on a particularly busy road and in our arrogant innocence had thought his hay meadow was a part of the verge. A farmer I met in Dobrovăț near the Prut River told me he was eating his own seed corn, not from profligacy but necessity, because he could not afford to buy any more. And further south, in the outskirts of Vaslui, generations of families were hoeing their fields in the cruel mid-day sun. They barely raised their heads as we went by.

Satul Nou is a ramshackle village on the bald, hot plateau near Iaşi. We riders rested there to water our ponies and quench our own thirsts, and let go momentarily of personal grievances to watch homesteaders skilfully making their own construction material. They were using 'chirpici' (pronounced 'keerpeech'), adobe bricks made from mud that is taken from the edges of ponds, then mixed with straw and dried in the sun. The bricks were large, measuring about eighteen by eight by eight inches. Once set, they provided solid walls and good insulation; the traditional method of facing them would have been to cover them with lime plaster, but nowadays householders used concrete to keep the rain out, so that the walls could not breathe. We saw half-finished buildings everywhere: some were meant to be office blocks but most were private houses. They revealed a wonderfully ad-hoc mixture of materials. Some of them comprised brick, wood and concrete in the same structure. Others looked as though they had been inspired by Byzantine churches: two rows of concrete alternated with one of brick. It made a pleasing pattern that would eventually be lost to sight, convincing me that the builders had a natural feeling for aesthetics no matter whether what they created would be on show or not.

The small communities of farmers and craftsmen that were once Moldavia's backbone have been chopped about. They seem demoralised to an extent that makes Maramureş look like the epitome of social cohesion. Ancient rural customs and folklore have become fragmented as well. This may be a legacy of Ceauşescu's interest in the Maramureş. It could also be due to the fact that Moldavia is not an isolated mountain plateau but a corridor between central Asia and western Europe. Migrating peoples have used it for thousands of years, creating a multiethnic mix of Vlachs (as medieval Europeans used to call Romanians), Slavs, Tartars, Turks, Armenians, Jews, Greeks, not to speak of smaller enclaves of Huţuls, Csangö and Lipoveni, upon the older vestiges of Sarmatians, Scythians and Thracians. The Ottoman Turks, the Habsburgs, the Russians and later the Soviet Union cut off slices of Moldavia leaving this country, like the insanely belligerant knight in 'Monty Python and the Holy Grail', headless and armless but still fighting.

A Moldavian paradox

While Stephen was famed as a brilliant and decisive leader, Moldavians have a reputation for being dreamy by nature and backward
by circumstance. In a sense they are to other Romanians what the
Irish are to the English, the butt of sentimental affection and pa-
tronising jokes. Like most generalisations such a reputation falls
short of the truth. Moldavia is the seat of what was once the country's greatest cultural capital, Iași (Jassy to the English). To its
credit are several of the greatest writers and musicians that Romania has ever produced. Among them are the Romantic poet and political reformer, Mihai Eminescu, the novelist Mihail Sadoveanu and
the composer George Enescu.

Moldavia and Moldova are two different places and also the
same one: the former is the word that English speakers use for the
medieval Romanian principality which Bogdan founded back in the
14th century and is now the north-eastern part of Romania; the latter is the Romanian name for that same principality and the international name of the post-soviet republic which lies to the east of
Moldavia across the Prut River. The Moldovan Republic covers
much of the area that was once known as Bessarabia, and seventy
percent of the Moldovan Republic's population speak Romanian as
their first language. Confused?

Câmpulung Moldovenesc

On the way to meet the film crew in Sucevița, I called in to see some
friends in Câmpulung Moldovenesc. Marcel was the director of the
town's Wood Museum. The museum, containing agricultural and
fishing tools, traps, furniture, household tools, musical instruments,
ceremonial artefacts and the largest spoons I had ever seen – they
were big enough to hold a baby - occupied several floors of a
gloomy, Neo-Classical building on the main street. The museum
could have done with a coat of paint, but the bonus was that I had
the place to myself and could marvel, dream and speculate my way
through the series of displays like a child in her grandparents' attic.
A discreet museum assistant turned the lights off behind me but did
not hassle me; saving electricity was high on the daily agenda, but
so was the wish to make people feel at ease.

Marcel was a large, genial person who seemed out of place in
a position where tight-faced bureaucrats have become the norm. He
was devoted to the museum and the region's folk culture; as we
walked round together his enthusiasm, shining through the dingy
exhibition rooms, provided the main source of light.

Ortensia taught French at a local high school and complained bitterly about the lack of the most basic books; in an unprecedented move the teachers were going on strike, fed up with continual promises that were never fulfilled. She was charming and vivacious and fluttered round her bear-like husband like a butterfly. Both of them treated me like an honoured guest, even though I frequently turned up unannounced. They lived in a four-bedroomed first floor flat with their two nearly grown-up children and a noisy Siamese cat. In the backyard, Marcel grew vegetables and roses in a perfectly geometrical, perfectly weedless garden the size of a man's handkerchief. Cherry trees bordered two sides. They had neither flowered nor fruited that year.

"It's because of the bombing in Kosovo," Marcel told me. "The fallout is so toxic it is killing the cherries." His face was unnaturally red as if to make up for the loss. Marcel had a severe heart problem and was treating it with gnarled white roots dug up from some woodland he owned in the mountains. This was no new age fad but a resort to natural remedies in the absence of anything else. On their combined salaries the couple could not afford conventional drugs.

A pocket of Celts

In the museum's loft there are shelves-full of embroidered linen women's blouses and wide men's belts patterned with thousands of small coloured beads. They are going musty from lack of funds to care for them. Some of the blouses were made by the Huțuls. The Huțuls are descendants of the Celts who live in the mountainous regions between Moldavia, Maramureș and Ukraine. They are supposed to have red hair and freckles like the Scots, although I never saw one close enough to check. Their language is a Slavonic dialect. Huțuls were brilliant metalworkers and there is a 19th century ceremonial hatchet on display in the museum. Along the length of the handle is a woven decoration, identical to that on the blouses. I had seen the same pattern on Celtic crosses in Wales. Sadly their skills in this craft have died out, but the Huțuls have survived in a few small pockets. There are maybe some twenty thousand of them left and they have kept their own particular customs for birth and burial.

Huțuls have been forgotten like the breeds of sheep and goats they once raised, and their name is more often associated with the sure-footed mountain ponies which are bred at the national Huțul stud at Lucina. In the 1960s, Kosei Miya once saw a Huțul man walking from northern Maramureş to Baia Mare in a suit made entirely of leaves.

Breathless in Suceviţa

Angela Gheorghiu has a superb, lyric soprano voice and incredible breath control. She is also a great beauty with long, raven hair and perfect features. Angela was born in the town of Adjud in north central Moldavia where her father worked as a railway official. She began performing on stage at the age of five and trained in Bucharest under Marin Constantin, the grand old man of Romania's classical music scene. The Revolution came at the right time for her, and allowed her to continue her career abroad unchecked by the political barriers that had stood in the way of predecessors. Angela's debut at Covent Garden as Violetta in 'La Traviata' was so powerful that the opera house extended the season. It was her capacity to switch in the fraction of a second from blowing your ears out to wooing them gently with a melodious pianissimo that set her apart from everyone else.

Angela had never seen the painted churches of Bucovina. She had the idea of making a film about them and the music that was connected with them. A chance meeting with BBC producer Jonathan Fulford brought the idea to fruition. The story line was simple: Angela would jet into Bucharest for a nostalgic homecoming and introduce these unique buildings to an English-speaking audience. She would also take the leading role in a programme of Byzantine, classical and Romanian folk music with the churches and Bucovina's fairy-tale landscapes as her background. The film was to be made jointly with Romanian television.

There was a chance she might cancel because of nerves. In the event, she showed herself to be part of the team and made the experience fun for everyone. She does not speak English easily, and presenting the film as well as being its main focus was tricky. After the Aleutian she was flying in to Suceava had to return to Bucharest, she refused go by air again, which infuriated the BBC managers but endeared her to me. If God had meant us to fly, he would have given us rubber bodies. She arrived in Bucovina by road, trailing a retinue that consisted of her husband the Italian tenor Roberto Alagna, her mother, a couple of nieces, a secretary, an agent, dressers, make-up artistes and seamstresses, her former singing teacher, Marin Constantin, and Madrigal, the Romanian national choir.

Some of the last scenes in the film were made in Suceviţa at night. Suceviţa is the largest and most splendid of all the painted churches. It was lit as though the moon were shining through its windows. The nuns, who had kept out of the way all day, relaxed, kneeling down like decorous ravens wherever they could find a free space among the cameras, lights and cables. They were savouring the experience of seeing their hallowed sanctuary used for a purpose that was in keeping with its dignity, in the hope that they might appear on television too.

My rôle came at the end of the film; I was to be a visiting expert who could describe what was going on in the glorious paintings that enveloped Sucevița. It was here that the exotic 16th century flowering came to an end, disappearing in the 1590s as abruptly as, some seventy years beforehand, it had started.

In the immediacy of filming, it was hard to tell who was more nervous, Angela Gheorghiu, the nuns or me. Having hung around for hours in Sucevița's churchyard trying to hide my camera and an ostentatious tripod, I was irritated. Media people, I thought bitterly; everything has to wait for them. Terrified that I would forget all the information I had prepared, my mouth became very dry.

Out of nerves I shushed Jonathan Fulford when he arrived and shouted a friendly greeting to me across the churchyard – I had been taught that you must not make scenes in such places. Hand outstretched, he took it in his stride; the man had dedicated months of preparation to this trip and he was absolutely certain of what he wanted and how to get it. Sucevița became a film set instead of a monastery. The choir members lounged around looking elegant and haughty, the men in dinner suits and bow ties and the women in long white frocks covered with embroidered, sleeveless overdresses that were open at the front and fell down to the ground. The men casually practised Byzantine plain song in the naos; the sound resonated into the high domes forty feet above us and raised the hairs on the back of my neck.

Reluctantly I allowed the Romanian crew manager to put make-up on my face; she told me she was a professional producer acting as back-up. She had plans to make a soap opera about the country's greatest legends that would wow audiences all over Romania. We did our takes inside and outside the church, focussing on the Ladder of Virtue, the Jesse Tree and the Menologion. Angela Gheorghiu made a brave effort to look interested and I managed to avoid giggling.

After we had finished the painting sequence, Angela Gheorghiu stood on a stone balcony overlooking the great church courtyard and the members of Madrigal arranged themselves on a wooden gangway which ran along the monastery wall beside it. Looking down on us, diva and choir sang a folk carol called Floricica (The Little Flower):

Floricica, floricea
Ce eşti mândra ca o stea
Ce eşti mândra ca o stea

Vezi aici pe braţul meu
Ţi-l aduc pe Dumnezeu
Ţi-l aduc pe Dumnezeu

Floricica se-nchina
Şi miresme-i aducea
Şi miresme-i aducea

Şi eu mica floricea
Ţi aduc inima mea
Ţi aduc inima mea

('Floricica, little flower,
You are as proud as a star;
Look here in my arms
I am bringing you Lord Jesus;
Floricica bent her head
And put forth a lovely scent;
And I also, little flower,
I am bringing you my heart')

It was a relief to find that Angela Gheorghiu could laugh at herself. We saw this when, haloed in pink silk with the spotlight full on her, she glided solemnly down the aisle, miming her pre-recorded aria in take after frustrating take, only to collapse in mock exasperation as soon as she turned the corner and was out of shot.

A nun's life

Ecaterina was in her late twenties, the youngest of three sisters from the same family who had all become nuns at Suceviţa. She worked as a guide, and every afternoon between two and five she made herself available to show visitors around the church. Ecaterina wanted to learn English, and she had started teaching herself from an odd collection of books purloined from friends and tourists. She helped to find me somewhere to stay in the village, and afterwards agreed to share her knowledge about the paintings so that I could bone up before filming. Later, we sat in the shade of the pretty, square, porticoed porch on the north side of the church, near the frescos which show the Ladder of Virtue, the mysteriously heretical Adam's Contract with the Devil, and the Life of St. Nicholas. The inside of the porch was painted with fresh, wispy flowers and vegetation in yellow and green like the designs on the local Kuty pottery; its opposite number on the south side was not an exact twin but had different porticos and exuberant paintings of the Apocalypse. A zigzag band of gold-coloured paint bordered two of the arches on the southern porch, echoing the form and colour of Brâncuşi's Column of the Infinite, the 100-ft high iron and steel tower that he designed for the town of Târgu Jiu as a war memorial in 1937.

Ecaterina was reading a heavily abridged version of 'The Wind in the Willows' and she pulled the copy out of a pocket. Her hands were mottled with chilblains even though it was August.

"It is stupid," she said, giving vent to feelings that had been building up as we walked around together, "I need to know English because we have so many English-speaking visitors. But there is no way of getting lessons here. Can't you help me? I want to do this so much." I promised to contact an Orthodox bishop in Oxford in case he could help her find a place on a language course, and suggested she write to the British Council in Bucharest. The next morning I went to a service in the 'paraclis', a little, barrel-vaulted chapel with two aisles built into the fortified walls of Suceviţa's compound. The nuns used it mainly for themselves and could worship here without the intervention of a male priest. For some reason I had been affected by the friendly, caring atmosphere which the nuns generated, and sitting with them as they prayed was a way of acknowledging the tolerance with which they had treated me. Prayers had begun an hour before I arrived and the session would go on for another four. Nuns in various stages of devotion were sitting on wooden benches or kneeling on the floor, wherever they felt most comfortable. They were from all stages of life too, from rosy-cheeked teenagers to hobbling octogenarians. Some were bent double, their crumpled bodies abandoned to arthritis and piety. They took turns to read from a lectern, and every so often one of them would glide out, genuflecting and crossing herself in decorous silence, and others would drift in. In their blackness they looked severe, but they were not zombies.

Ecaterina told me that since the Revolution many teenage girls had chosen to enter nunneries rather than face a life of uncertainty. It was very hard, disciplined work, with long hours spent farming, cleaning and preparing food. She looked amazed when I suggested becoming a nun might be a way of avoiding reality. Ecaterina had her sisters with her and in her terms the choice she had made was not such a bad one. Except that she was unhappy now, with the limitations of her life and her frozen hands.

A facelift for the Church Fathers

Sucevița was undergoing a transition: its abbess had recently died and as yet no-one had been appointed in her place. Meanwhile, Ecaterina's oldest sister, Margareta, was acting as head. Her middle sister, Elena, was a qualified picture restorer who was helping to clean the frescos in the dome. Thanks to Ecaterina, Elena gave me a personal conducted tour of the paintings, and we climbed the wooden scaffolding when no-one else was around to object.

The crisp shapes and glowing colours that had blazed from the walls in the 1590s were re-emerging from centuries of blackness. Test areas had been left on the walls to show how much dirt had been taken off. As we climbed up the spiral staircase which connected the five platforms of the scaffold tower, Elena explained the scenes in the spandrels and lunettes, finishing at the top with the most important figures in the hierarchy, the Apostles and the Evangelists. The artists had taken as much care in the most inaccessible, invisible reaches of the church as they had at normal eye level.

"There were about thirty painters," Elena told me, "and they were organised into separate teams, each of which specialised in different areas: architecture or figures or landscapes for example. There were master artists in charge of them, but the overall responsibility for the composition of the frescos belonged to Egumen Gheorghe Movilă, one of the founders, who became a bishop."

I bought a fat Romanian-English dictionary for Ecaterina and wrote to Oxford. I got no reply. Months went by and the next time I went to Sucevița, Margareta gave me some news: the previous winter when it had been exceptionally cold Ecaterina had fallen ill so badly that her kidneys had been affected. Since then she had decided to join a group of Romanian nuns who had reopened a monastery on Cyprus. I was sorry not to see her again.

Painted churches

The images I had seen in Maramureș churches were so compelling that they remained fixed in my mind's eye long after I crossed into Moldavia. They were crude by comparison with the superbly painted figures on the walls of Bucovina's monasteries, and yet the combination of bright colours, compositional rhythms and graphic narratives in both places imprinted themselves forcefully on my imagination. I wondered if the ideas they embodied could possibly be used as a counterpoint to the destructive effects of modernisation. The paintings were meant to carry a political as well as a religious message and the Church's bureaucracy was heavily involved. I was like a child with its nose pressed to a gorgeous shop window; I envied the paintings' apparent certainties, and it felt cold outside.

There are six painted churches that belong to the 'must see' category in Bucovina: Voroneț, Humor, Moldovița, Arbore, Sucevița and Probota. A few more of the original twenty-two still exist, but their external paintings have worn away altogether or are only visible in faint patches. The extraordinary thing about the best six is that, bar the weathering on the north side, almost every scene is clear and its colouring bright.

The quality and vitality of the Voroneț paintings stand out from the others. A stunning azurite blue – known as Voroneț blue - forms the background to all the 'earthly' scenes on the outer walls. I wanted to photograph them, and having a camera, tripod, and some slow film with me, the opportunity was too good to miss. It

was not to be. The 'Stareța' (Abbess) of Voroneț surprised me by saying that as an unbeliever I was not welcome to study the church. It was a sign of the head-on conflict which famous monasteries like Voroneț are having to face everyday: they need the income which tourists bring, but the sisters feel threatened by having to admit heathen bodies onto their hallowed ground. After all, these are working institutions first, and visitor attractions second. Some monasteries were coping with this dual role better than others – Moldovița had the brilliant Maica Elena, and in fact Voroneț had an excellent guide in Sister Gabriela - but at that time my request, coming so suddenly and unsupported by letters of recommendation carrying the appropriate stamps, cut its senior management to the quick. My request for help met with the rebuke that I had no right to information because I was not 'a lover of icons'. I had to be content with snapping the paintings freehand like everyone else.

Inside the frescos were being cleaned and wooden scaffolding obscured most of the scenes in the naos. But the exonarthex, an extension built specifically to carry external paintings at the west end, contained marvellous pictures of ancient saints, including Elijah in his chariot. A sister who was on duty by the entrance selling candles and promises of prayers, grudgingly admitted that the scenes were from the Menologion, the Orthodox Calendar, which traditionally began on the first of September, and illustrated the martyrdoms of every saint in the canon. Each month was separated by an anthropomorphic image of a moon.

The amazing blue of Voroneț comes to its climax on the south wall, where a central panel illustrates the Tree of Jesse, Jesus's family tree. Isaiah (Jesse) lies at the bottom, like the venerable root stock of a tree of life, and the scene opens out above him into a trellis of unfolding flower heads on curling stems. Each one encircles a vignette; the vignettes span the Old and New Testaments, and show a poetic if politically-motivated licence, including pre-Christian scholars, kings and philosophers such as Plato, Aristotle and Sophocles to emphasise the intellectual authority of the Church.

An unsolved puzzle

No-one has fully explained why the churches should have been painted outside at this particular time and in this particular place. There are other Orthodox churches with external frescos in Greece and Macedonia. They are not nearly so magnificent as the ones in Bucovina, but for all I know this practice was a feature of Byzantine churches elsewhere too. Learned scholars have pointed to the stonework on Romanesque cathedrals in France as one possible source for the idiom, and on Orthodox churches in Kiev as another. With its tent-like roof and dazzling azure walls, the south wall of Voroneţ looks like an oriental pavilion. When I saw them the first thing that sprang to my mind was an image of the east: Persian carpets and miniatures, the floral tiles on the blue Timurid mosques in Herat, the ivans of Isfahan.

Stephen the Great came to the Moldavian throne in 1437 and built his churches at a time when the Timurid Renaissance was in full swing. Most art historians believe that the external paintings were begun during the reign of his son, Petru, in the 1530s, but there is a theory that the first frescos appeared at the end of Stephen's reign, in the 1490s. One of Stephen's wives was Maria of Mangop, a Tartar princess from the Crimea. Cultural influences leap over political barriers and cover great geographical distances: Byzantium influenced Islamic art and vice versa, before, during and after Mehmed's conquest of Constantinople. Is it possible that some visiting diplomat from Persia or Afghanistan inspired the Muşatin princes to emulate the beautiful mosques and ivans of Persia, or that a merchant from Moldavia was so bowled over by the sight of them that he rushed home to tell his prince? The most prosaic explanations can often be the most realistic: maybe an Armenian trader wanted to off-load a consignment of azurite that was surplus to requirements.

Connective tissue

There is to my knowledge no manual that explains every scene to visitors, not even to the Orthodox ones. When I returned a year later, Sister Gabriela explained the imagery in the most famous fresco of all. This is The Last Judgment, which fills the entire outer west wall. In a world strictly divided into good and evil, there are signs of pagan beliefs and a love of folklore. While Moldavian art may have come late on the Byzantine scene, the artists of Voroneţ were no lesser practitioners than their Greek or Macedonian forerunners. They were trained in the same traditions, and served their apprenticeships in professional workshops in the medieval capital of Suceava and the monastery of Putna. Voroneţ's frescos were painted by masters of their art form, and the composition on the west wall hangs together superbly well. The seriousness of the subject is never in doubt, but their delight in the scenes dealing with Hell, the Revival of Dead Souls, and the Spirit of the Sea who rides on a dolphin, shows a human side that makes the fresco much more accessible.

On the north-west buttress of the church, and on the north wall, are the faded remains of other narrative sequences. They include a painting of a spiral staircase, a version of the symbolic ladder of virtue which I had seen a few years earlier in Călineşti. The staircase is known as the Customs Post at Heaven's Gate and the basic idea, that monks must pass a series of rigorous moral tests before arriving in Paradise, is the same. But I had never seen or heard of it before and was hungry for more examples of unusual Christian stories in a rural context. Voroneţ was abandoned during the Habsburg and communist periods. Setting their reservations aside, the nuns have brought it to life again. Those like Sisters Elena and Gabriela are working to create a symbiotic connection between working shrine and historic monument. They will have to work fast. Because earlier restorers used concrete pointing, water is collecting in the walls behind the paintings. If no action is taken, they may start to fall off and these astonishing scenes will be lost to believers and heathens alike.

Study break

Curious to know more, I tried to find some answers in Iaşi. The city is home to Romania's oldest university, the former cultural capital and a reluctant cultural backwater. I met Ioan, a chain-smoking professor of medieval history, who was buried under high-rise paper stacks in his faculty office. Ioan answered my questions with the briskness that comes from years of dealing with callow students. Which books would he recommend as an introduction to the churches' iconography? He dictated a list as long as my arm. "Next question?" Where could I find people to tell me about Adam's Contract and its connection with the Bogumil heresy? He fired off some names, addresses and phone numbers. "Next question?" I did not have one: I needed to read.

Waving goodbye to the professor through a smokey, philosophical haze, I walked up two flights of stairs to the faculty library. Term had not started and the librarians gave me their undivided attention; once I had handed over my passport the place was mine from eight in the morning until four in the afternoon. Rows of beech tables and high-backed chairs filled the main reading room, and on the high window-sills were pots of well-tended cacti, begonias and bizzy-lizzies. The librarians were chatty; they wanted to know what I thought of the government's decision not to return Castle Peleş to ex-King Michael.

I did not find answers but more questions. The books and articles I read were fascinating, but there was a huge conceptual gap between the authors' standpoints and mine: they were believers and I was not – at least not an Orthodox Christian; they were writing at a time when Romania was communist and I was not, nor had I any experience of living under such a regime.

Every time I brought up the connection between the Bogumils and Adam's Contract, Romanian churchmen denied it. The Bogumils had originated in Armenia, and Armenians were anathema because they were monophysites (they believed in the single person of God). Armenians were among the damned on the west wall of Voroneț. Yet Armenians had been to 16th and 17th century Romania what the Jews were to become: diplomats and merchants, fixers who smoothed the way, translators, middlemen. An Armenian even became prince of Moldavia for a while, and there were splendid Armenian churches in Suceava, Iași and Bucharest.

As I understood it the Bogumils had brought their puritanical fundamentalism to eastern Europe. Thence it had spread to the west, affecting Albigensians and like organisations whose adherents were disgusted at the venality of the official church. They wanted to go back to basics. In retaliation the Roman Catholic Church initiated the Inquisition. If there were a connection between the paintings on the churches of Bucovina and Bogumilism, it must have come about through the spread of folk culture, of which the story of Adam's Contract with the Devil was probably a popular example. Stephen's son, Petru Rareș, was illegitimate; he had been born to an educated country woman in Hârlău, a town between Iași and Suceava, near Stephen's Cotnari vineyards on the Moldavian plateau. Petru was responsible for the most famous painted frescos and keen to establish his position as the great prince's rightful heir. If his mother had taught him the story at her knee, he might well have wanted to see it repeated on his churches' walls.

Adam's Contract appears at Voroneț and on the walls of Sucevița, the monastery which was built by descendants of Petru's father and mother, the Movilă family. It is a cautionary tale about Adam after the Fall, when he delved and Eve span. The Devil gives Adam permission to cultivate the land on condition that in payment Adam promises to give the Devil complete power over his children. At the moment when Adam is about to sign the agreement, Christ appears and admonishes him, and the Devil is sent packing. Christ tells Adam that he is doomed but his descendants will have the chance to make a choice between good and evil.

What influence do these paintings have on Romania's contemporary artists? I had a chance to find out when I met Matei, a conceptual artist who lectures at the art college in Iași. He looks like an angel by Michelangelo. Since Romania opened its doors, Matei has travelled all over the world, taking part in exhibitions as far

110

apart as Istanbul and Chicago, Belgrade and Dublin. In the early 1990s he founded a biennial art show called Periferic, which has the same meaning in Romanian as it does in French. With the 'centres' of contemporary art lying undisputably in the West - New York, London, Paris, Amsterdam, Los Angeles - Moldavian artists feel they are marginal. Matei wanted to highlight this fact and turn it to their advantage. The biennale happens over four days and takes place in the old, semi-derelict Turkish baths below the Orthodox Cathedral. It has grown: actions and videos, performances and light-shows are all a part of the package, throwing the concept of a 'centre' and its 'satellites' into question. Communications technology makes a nonsense of distances: most of us can talk to each other instantly by e-mail these days.

"I've given up making art for managing it!" Matei said while we sat in his studio in the run-down block built for sculptors in the 1970s. "I've become Mr. Big Mouth instead, but that's what we need here, unfortunately." He grinned at the irony. Stacked around the high white walls were posters and photographs, bits of collage and 3-D props for installations. What did he think of Romania's cultural heritage, and the painted churches? (I was sure he would dismiss them.) "They are incredibly important for us," he said, giving me a shock. "We need a sense of continuity, specially our young people. It would be a tragedy if all these things were destroyed; life would become meaningless... This country is in a mess; our artists are terribly confused. The state does not support them any more; they feel cut-off and directionless. The old things, the good things, like the painted churches, our history and our folklore, give us something to hold onto." That was another reason why artists (and people in general) felt isolated in Iaşi: the spectre of a Russian, or even an Asiatic, invasion, however unlikely in the 1990s, was an unspoken fear that many shared; it had been part of their history for so long. Ex Oriente Lux was the title of an art exhibition held in Bucharest after the Revolution, but - if you believed the politicians and bankers - the light of the future came from the west, not the east. Viewed like this, Iaşi seemed to be teetering on the edge of an abyss.

We visited a Roma village called Ciurea. Statistically the Roma comprise about ten percent of Romania's population, and their presence is a sore which many 'gadgé' (non-Roma) could happily do without. They are listed among the eighteen or so official ethnic minorities who live in Romania today, but in spite of brave efforts on both sides they are as far from assimilation as they have ever been. In their terms, they have as much right to be heard as anyone else; Roma have lived in these lands since the 14th century.

They are the constant reminder of a traffic in human lives which began under prince Mircea cel Bătrân (Mircea the Wise) of

Wallachia and continued with Stephen the Great in Moldavia. They imported scores of gypsies who were tied to their property and had to work as slaves. Sometimes these princes would give thirty or forty families as a gift to a monastery. In purely aesthetic terms they bring gaiety and colour to countryside and town alike, and no journey through Romania would be complete without seeing them.

The majority live in abject poverty, but since the Revolution, wealthy Gypsies have been building palaces. These houses are outrageously, gloriously kitsch. Often three or four storeys high, they have shiny zinc roofs which are tiered, turreted and filigreed like lace. They have balconies on all but the ground floor and the outside walls are clad in something that looks like crazy-paving. It comes in a variety of hues including grey, white, pink and red. Inside they have marble staircases and glass chandeliers and alongside these opulent, western Baroque-style furnishings, there are cheap nylon tapestries depicting tiger hunts and 'off the shelf' sofas with plush magenta coverings. Houses like these are going up all over Romania. Usually they are the isolated palaces of the 'bulibashi' (the Roma kings) but in some cases there are clusters of them crammed together in new villages. Seeing these lordly buildings huddled together cheek by jowl at the end of a dirt track only adds to their incongruity. They have become popular with tourists, and parties of eager Dutch and Belgian visitors can sometimes be seen snapping the Roma mansions from the safety of their intercontinental coaches. It is not from fear of being attacked that they stay inside, but because they know that the Roma will charge them for the privilege if they do not.

The odd thing is that the Roma prefer not to live in their amazing houses, but leave them empty, as showcases. Their real homes are shacks pitched somewhere within easy shouting distance of the baronial front doors. Doberman pinschers and German shepherd dogs patrol their properties and keep you away from the fleets of expensive and well-valeted cars lined up six abreast. Gypsy women have their status symbols too. Sometimes they put their skirts on display, piling the needle-pleated, parrot-coloured crêpe circles one on top of another in competition with their neighbours.

In a suburb of Iaşi I found Caterina, a medical doctor who made a point of treating Roma women. She had had some success in persuading them to take contraceptives.

"I get on with them OK," she said. "The main problem is their husbands: having lots of children is a sign of virility and status." Caterina stuck out from her down-trodden surroundings. She was a pillar of strength and humanity. I found her cultural awareness and her tolerance astonishing. Caterina was able to articulate concepts and feelings which left me far behind. Her husband wanted to move to the USA; she would have none of it. "My work is here," she told me with quiet determination. I could not help wondering if she were Jewish; I thought it might explain her sympathy with the Roma. Iaşi's Jews had been down-trodden too.

Iaşi has an acknowledged 'Gypsy problem'. Five years after I met Caterina, in the same month that I saw Ciurea, the city council announced it had plans to build a district outside the city exclusively for Roma. Opinion was divided between those who saw this as a form of ghettoisation and others who were fed up with living next to people who indulged in drunken brawls and crime. Weeks later I returned to Iaşi. On the night I arrived, my friends' nanny's fiancé was attacked and killed in the stairwell of a block of flats a quarter of a mile from their house. An old woman had seen the murder; too frightened to help, she told the police that a group of six or seven Gypsies had set upon the boy, stabbed him with knives and broken bottles and run away. The reason was appallingly trivial. A friend of his had driven into town with a Roma woman earlier that day and her jealous boyfriend had wreaked his vengeance on the nearest gadgé he could find. The old woman would not testify in court.

I left with the feeling that there are two cities called Iaşi, one educated, civilised and full of promise, the other lawless and frightening. I hoped I was wrong, that the impression was subjective and therefore of no weight. But I could not see how the city's social problems would be solved by its enormous, state of the art shopping mall and the international airport that was expected to open in 2002.

Into the Black Forest

Vrancea is an area of south-west Moldavia. It encompasses sandy, vine-rich plains and the high Carpathians as they bend south from Bucovina and then west again, parallel to the Danube. Once it was covered in dense woodland which gave the region its name: Vrancea means The Black Forest. Black was not a colour I would have associated with Vrancea's blazing copper Fall, but if they go there at all, foreign tourists stick to the vineyards; disgorging from coaches to accept a protocol tour of the freezing cellars, a ceremonial lunch and back to the bus again to sleep it off as they ride north on the next leg of their whistlestop trip. Vrancea is reputed to be where the folktale, Miorița, originated: the 19th century poet Vasile Alecsandri claimed to have adapted it from an oral tradition which survived in Soveja, high in the mountains. Miorița has many versions in eastern Europe, but Vrancea remains little known.

It is an earthquake zone, and prone to landslides, but the mountains are ravishing. I went there with Cristina, a friend from Bucharest, when she was collecting data for her job at the Village Museum. We took a bus into the Vrancea Sub-Carpathians from Focşani, the county town. Squashed into our seats, we rode through the slush of a November day with the wheels sliding and spinning and the doors half open. Most of the way, we had to put up with the unwelcome attentions of a drunk who kept nudging us with his elbows and making lewd suggestions. When we fell out of the bus at the entrance to Negrileşti village, three hours had gone by and it was nearly dark. Smoke was curling upwards from blackened roofs; I thought they were on fire. Cristina laughed, rather recklessly I thought. I knew we English were security-mad, but surely this was an emergency? There was no need to panic. The spiralling fumes coming through the shingles were no accident: it was the way villagers smoked their meat. They hung the joints from the rafters and their chimneys funnelled the heat into that space, rather than outside to the open air. We walked the mile into Negrileşti and followed our noses to a bakery: hot, fresh white loaves were on sale for a few pennies. We bought one each and ate them there and then, pulling off great hunks to stave our hunger. As we made our way into the village the style of the houses changed from modern brick villas to handsome, well-proportioned wattle and daub buildings with verandahs. I noticed the posts were square, straight and slender, not like the ones in Maramureş at all.

Cristina had come to see a young woodworker called Toma; we were to stay in his parents' house for the night. Toma had made a collection of traditional clothes which he was anxious to sell to the museum. He had piles of embroidered, wrap-around woollen skirts in his workshop, and long woven belts to hold them in place. The material was dense and dark with strands of gold and silver thread to lighten it; it felt good to the touch. Toma's own work was traditional too: he made cheese dollies and butter moulds, using old patterns which he sometimes adapted to his own whim. The dollies were in two pieces of rectangular wood, slightly waisted in the middle, that slotted together to hold a viscous dollop of liquid cheese; each section had raised and incised geometrical designs on their inner surfaces, and these would appear in negative when the cheese was set. Toma brought us

Tipar de caş
(Cheese dolly)

to visit an aunt who showed us how she heated the cheese in metal saucepans, and when it was the right consistency poured it onto one half of the dolly and pressed the other into it. Cheese splurged out all around the wooden presses but that did not matter; we ate it off. The cheese was a delicious 'caşcaval' (pron. 'cashcaval'), quite like English cheddar but chewier and more tangy.

Toma had plans. He wanted to get funding for a sports and tourist village outside Negrileşti. The village would be constructed in wood, in the local way, and have all kinds of modern facilities. All he needed was a grant to set it on its way. He was also the village vet, and as we walked to his parents' house in the lightly swirling snow, someone rushed up to him and called him away. A farrowing pig was in trouble in a nearby village; Toma made his apologies and vanished. We did not see him again until early the next morning when he appeared, purple-faced and glowing from an all-night drinking session.

Cristina and I walked through Negrileşti; we went to the forge where two sweating brothers were slaving over the fire, grabbing semi-molten metal rods to make ironwork gates, window guards and horseshoes; we visited a miller-cum-carpenter's yard where row upon row of arcane, old-fashioned implements hung from nails on a timber wall like an installation by a conceptual artist. A clanking electric knife-grinding belt wobbled on its frame and everything was covered in a layer of sawdust, like a monochrome print. The miller-cum-carpenter wore a tall lambskin hat; he was rushed off his feet, but grudgingly consented to let me take his photograph against the wall of his barn; in my underexposed slide, his unsmiling face is the colour of sawdust too. Toma's uncle was building himself a new house: he was using wattle and daub to make the walls. The wattle was made from slender hazel stems and the daub was a thick brown sauce of cowdung, mud and straw.

An old lady had just died in Negrileşti; we were invited to the funeral feast to share the special cakes which are made to commemorate the dead, and drink ţuica and wine. We did not know the people, but they would not take no for an answer; this was their way of overcoming grief and moving on. Outside in the garden was a row of trestle tables covered in white cloths. There were piles of food and drink on the tables, and beside them, some of the dead person's clothes had been tied to a tree: handkerchiefs and scarves which tradition believed she might need in the next world.

The next time we saw him, Toma's concentration had evaporated. All his creative enthusiasm seemed to have flown out of the window too. Drink or despair had got the better of him. When we left he escorted us blearily to the bus stop outside a bar on the main road to Focşani. We sat primly inside while he downed a couple of beers. Toma flung an arm round Cristina's shoulders:

"Caroline's very quiet today. Has she fallen in love with me?"

We missed the bus but caught a lift in a passing Dacia, on our way back to dull civilisation and days measured out in office jobs. Toma waved at us from the bar doorway, a bottle in his hand.

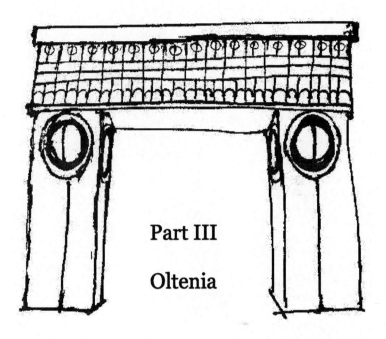

Part III

Oltenia

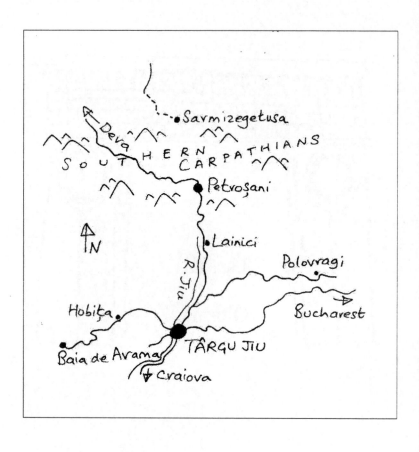

Oltenia was once part of the medieval principality of Wallachia. It lies between the Danube and the Southern Carpathians in south-west Romania. Oltenia's eastern limits come as far east as Argeş county, a beautiful agricultural area to the east of the Olt River. There is no formal boundary, but there the region merges with Muntenia, which encompasses the vineyards that export Dealul Mare wine, the oil fields and the river plain down to Bucharest. Together they form Wallachia. Oltenia is where the sculptor Constantin Brâncuşi was born which is why I wanted to see it so badly.

A Pilgrimage to Târgu Jiu

No other artist I know of has created such a dynamic marriage between modernity and the archaic. Brâncuşi inspired Modigliani and Mark Rothko and Isamu Noguchi. In Britain, Jacob Epstein, Barbara Hepworth, Henry Moore and Ben Nicholson were early converts and the land artist Andy Goldsworthy loves the photographs that Brâncuşi took in his own studio. As an art historian I was warned not to read too much into Brâncuşi's Romanian heritage. When I travelled around the county that seemed like a mean piece of nonsense: everywhere I went there were images that had Brâncuşi written all over them. Now this is not an art historical exegesis, but the sophisticated 'tree culture' which exists in Romania helped to give Brâncuşi his respect for the material, just as his training as a craftsman stood him in immeasurably good stead when he became a sculptor, and a 'real' artist. I was hungry for signs of his existence and in Gorj I looked out for shapes and textures that he would have known as a child. I was also hoping for signs that would increase my own sense of continuity and rootedness. The prosaic guide writer had a hidden agenda; the art historian wanted to drop her threadbare reserve. I longed for Brâncuşi, the man and his art, as though he had been my own grandfather. The old timber housing stock might be battered and swinging in the wind but there was plenty of material to feed the imagination. Never mind the doctoral thesis, here was the real thing.

Târgu Jiu is where Brâncuşi installed the three-piece war memorial that is dedicated to Romanian soldiers who died defending the town in 1917. It is a rough hotch potch of a place, on the edge of Romania's largest mining district. It was savaged by 'restructuring' in the 1960s and the modernist offices, shops and hotels that wiped out the rambling old streets look sorry for themselves. Târgu Jiu is currently the focus of a makeover which the World Monuments Fund has promised to support so that it will become a model of regeneration. Over the next thirty years the town centre will be redesigned to allow tourists to follow the Brâncuşi trail on its east to west axis; there will be more hotels and restaurants and parks, and it is hoped that businesses and tourists will flock there. For a while longer, fine old stone and brick buildings with handsome balconies and blind arcades and well-proportioned roofs stick out like ivory teeth in a mouth full of metal fillings. In the dog-eared park at the west end of town Brâncuşi's Table of Silence and Gate of the Kiss have been dismantled for repairs; so have the rectangular benches which lined the avenue between them. A footpath runs behind the empty circle where the Table stood. Beside it flows the River Jiu. In spate the river is a quarter-mile wide plate of lucent water that divides the 'cultural and commercial' centre from a district that has been set aside for the Roma. Looking across the divide one majestic evening, I saw the blue mountains in the distance under a salmon pink sky with gold-tinged clouds. In the flat-calm water were the reflections of the fantastic roofs of the Gypsy palaces. If I had half-closed one eye, I could have been in India beside the Ganges.

On the pretext of writing the guide, and later for articles and this book, I asked the prefecture of Gorj for help so that I could travel around looking at cultural sites. In fact I asked on three occasions and the county officials came up trumps every time. On the first visit I saw Brâncuşi's hundred-foot-tall Column of the Infinite, on the east side of Târgu Jiu, poking up like a black zigzag finger from a landscape covered in two feet of snow. I did not know that it was about to be taken down. For five years the seventeen rusty iron 'beads' which comprise the sculpture would lie waiting for officials and experts to make up their minds as to how and when it should be restored. My host was the director of Gorj county museum. It was a

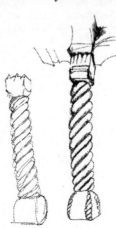

desperate time for him - salaries were falling while prices were rising - but he and his wife put me up on a camp-bed with every sign of friendliness.

A team of officials came with us for the jolly. We squashed into the museum's Dacia and headed north to Cârţişoară and its open air village museum. Rickety wooden gates with curving profiles and geometrical patterns, white-painted houses on stone bases with a timber storey and balconies, slender verandah posts that grew fatter towards the middle, verandah posts with twisted rope designs spiralling upwards; these buildings were like the ones I saw in Maramureş, but not

identical. They were adapted to a different climate, more riverine than alpine. The roofs were flatter, the horizontal and vertical rhythms more disciplined. I did not see shapes exactly like those found in Brâncuşi's columns but the connections were absolutely clear. We drove to Hobiţa, the village where Brâncuşi was born. It stands on flat terrain but the foothills are nearby. The sculptor's birthplace is a traditional cabin with a wide, steep roof and a verandah. There were carved patterns on
door frames and verandah posts. I
could not get over how small it was.
It had been moved from its original
location and turned into a museum.
When we went inside, I found
nothing to remind me of Brâncuşi.
There was no smell, just some rem-
nants of human habitation in a
sanitised display. What did I expect
after 70 years of absence? This was
better than nothing. Bleached wood
worn smooth with use and colourful woollen rugs; a narrow table
and some benches; small windows;

a few attractive pieces of rustic Gorj pottery: two small rooms for a family of nine. It was freezing. We went down the road for a ţuica with the director's friend. His house was like Brâncuşi's but warmer: we huddled round the iron stove in a kitchen armoured with enamel pots and pans. Voices hoarse with hard grind; faces red from the wind and brandy; good humoured-simplicity, unpretentiousness, a male-dominated society that shows an old-fashioned respect for women: this is Gorj as I remember it.

My next sight of the Column came in 2000. It was during the last few days of President Constantinescu's chaotic coalition. The iron beads had been cleaned and repaired, and were being carefully lowered onto the steel pillar that holds them up. They were a dull gold colour. Having cajoled the outgoing Minister of Culture for a pass, I watched the remaining beads being sandblasted and coated in the brass-alloy paint which had been formulated as closely as possible to the original specifications. I asked the engineers to let me climb the scaffold frame and, from somewhere near the level of the twelfth bead, watched the crane drivers and winching party per-form the delicate process of lifting and lowering the beads into place. They had been working non-stop for three months, rushing to get it finished before the new administration could claim the kudos. In spite of the pressure, the atmosphere was relaxed. I made the most of it, knowing the answer I would have received had I

asked to clamber in similar fashion over Anthony Gormley's Angel of the North. Controversy rumbled overhead: a prominent art historian said the work had been botched and would not last. Hundreds of thousands of tax-payers' dollars had been spent, and the wrangle continues.

There was an 'opening' party on 17 December 2000. I had an invitation to that too, and saw with pleasure how the event brought Gorjeni together. There were interminable waits for interminable speeches, and a lunatic in a helicopter buzzed low over our heads. When the protocol was finished, a rock band played with raucous energy and people jostled each other good-humouredly. Fathers swung baby daughters onto their shoulders for a better look. As dusk fell, the gleaming column became a maypole which had shed its streamers. It drew everyone's attention like a magnet. Seeing the crowd circling beneath it, I had the sensation that we were worshipping an ancient sun god.

During the two or three days that I stayed in Gorj I went back to Hobiţa. I had a look at the cemetery where members of Brâncuşi's family are buried. In place of headstones some of the graves had been marked by the felled trunks of fir trees. They had been pushed into the ground and were wrapped in ribbons. Nearby were the remains of a summer camp for sculptors. The artists' unions had encouraged this practice during the 1960s and 1970s and there were many others like it in the country elsewhere. Stumps of pale, lichen-softened stone carvings stood or lay abandoned in a rectangle of sparse woodland. Brâncuşi's influence was visible, but there was another which I recognised immediately: the blockish style that spoke of socialist realism and the communist ethos.

Exploring Gorj

I went back again to Gorj just after Iliescu fought off a challenge from the outrageous Vadim Tudor. Some of the personnel had changed, but the prefect and his colleagues made me feel welcome. I found myself wondering if British county officials would be as courteous. The prefect provided a car and driver for a day or two. In return I was expected only to show up for a few protocol meetings. A councillor invited me to lunch, and I found myself face to face with an Italian lawyer who told me most of his regular clients were mafiosi. Romania and Italy have a lot in common, but he wore an expensive-looking silk suit which seemed out of place in a country town where hip guys look like truck drivers on a Sunday outing. I stayed in the Hotel Gorj, a monstrous hard-edged hangover from the days of communist uniformity. My bedroom had dark maroon curtains that shut out all the light and, as if to underline its misery, I got food poisoning when I ate in the restaurant. To avoid the hotel during the evenings, I spent a lot of time in a poky internet café where crowds of teenage boys jostled for space at a few grimy computer terminals. When they started shoving me around too, I scarpered.

I recognised the diminutive driver, Ion, from my previous visit. He had kept his job, being low enough down the pecking order not to matter. He gave me the ghost of a smile which told me this better than words.

Gorj is a mining county and much of the landscape between Craiova and Târgu Jiu is scarred with quarry waste. Immediately to the north of Gorj lies the county of Hunedoara. Hunedoara contains the Jiu Valley, whence, during June 1990, belligerant miners came at Iliescu's behest to knock the stuffing out of students who had occupied University Square in Bucharest. The students were protesting peacefully about the failure of the new regime to embrace democracy. Afterwards the square was nicknamed Tiananmen. In 1997 the Jiu miners were on the move again, this time against the pit closures which the government was planning as part of its industrial modernisation programme. The miners were a powerful force, and their march towards Bucharest became front-page news; the threat of violence brought cabinet ministers scurrying out of the capital to talk about compromises and concessions. School teachers who had also been on strike for more pay and better conditions won nothing. A frightening image of the Jiu Valley miners lodged itself more deeply in my mind.

Gigantic power plants and scraggy fields in the Danube plain to the south of Gorj give way as you go north to the mellower, pastoral landscapes of the Carpathian foothills. Here lush beech forests and meadow-covered hillsides pull the eye and mind back from reality, shortening the view and making it more palatable. Romanian industry is in a parlous state. Its ugliness felt like an insult. Turning my back on it thankfully, I wondered which was more real, the grim landscape or the pretty one.

Thanks to the prefect of Gorj I visit the Mayor of a little town near Lainici monastery. Officially I am a 'mica delegaţia', a small delegation from England doing research into the culture of Gorj. I ask for details of the town's history. The Mayor, who looks terribly ill-at-ease, delves into some filing cabinets, and comes out with a faded fifty-page typescript from which he proceeds to read in a rapid, official voice. Having nothing better to do I take notes, finding later that I have put down how many houses are without water and gas: five percent in the first case, eighty percent in the second. If they have no gas, it means they have to heat their houses with wood-burning stoves or go cold. In flats with no chimneys, there is only one option. Italian furniture companies have invested heavily in Gorj; they are providing employment by turning trees into wood-chip. This is seen as a bright spot in an otherwise hopeless outlook.

We stop at Lainici, a modern monastery by Romanian standards. One church dates from the 18th and another from the late 20th century. The second church has breathtaking lines. Its porti-coed, marble porch is decorated in a style that is modelled on the Romanian Baroque: pierced stonework of interlocking vegetal forms. At the protocol lunch there are hand-picked local mush-rooms, fresh spring onions, recently killed meat and a home-made, amber-coloured brandy of such deliciousness that I am emboldened to ask the most impertinent questions. Such as why the Romanian Orthodox Church refuses to reveal the level of its collaboration with the security services during the Communist period. Surely it would help to clear the air and rid Romania of the pall of suspicion and resentment that hangs over it? The monk who is our host shows no animosity; with a charming, open smile, he tells me,

"It would not be a good idea; it would create an atmosphere of blame and retaliation."

The Mayor chips in:

"I was a pioneer when I was growing up; everybody joined the Party if they wanted a job. Does that mean I should be punished for it now?" The pioneers were a Communist Party institution rather like the British Boy Scouts, meant to instil the country's youth with a sense of collective responsibility and obedience to authority.

The car takes us further east on a road that runs parallel with the mountains. We take a side road into one of the bays of the bar-rage to see Polovragi Monastery. Underneath the porch at the west end is a thirty-foot long fresco showing the monasteries on Mount Athos. It is impossible to 'read' in one glance, and would be like a Chinese scroll painting except that the narrative is repetitive, not forward-moving. Row upon row of smooth, hump-backed pink and tan and grey hills march across the horizontal painting. Sprouting from each one are the pink and grey and tan buildings of the Athonite monasteries and hermitages. There are hundreds of them, from large clustered complexes to single huts that look no more complicated than a dog kennel. The buildings are similar but not identical - this is not wallpaper - and infinitesimal differences keep the eye busy looking for change and incident. There are onion-shaped domes and flat Greek ones, battlemented towers and walls with square or rounded entrances. In the gaps beside the monas-teries are figures of monks or itinerant hermits; either they are over life-size or the buildings are minute. Running right along the bot-tom edge of the fresco is a ribbon-like sea-way with ships on it. The fresco is a rhythmic pattern of hills, architecture, men and trees. At first its Byzantine style looks child-like, but the effect is cumulative. I feel dizzy after looking at it for five minutes.

Turning away from the painting to adjust to a 'normal' landscape, I rest my eyes on the sharp-edged Carpathian crags behind Polovragi. In the late afternoon sun I see them as pink and tan and grey.

With the cave-pocked mountains towering over us, the physical barrier between Wallachia and Transylvania begins to mean something. The socio-political one is showing some holes. In the village of Novaci, a brisker, less embarrassed-looking mayor tells me that Transylvanian shepherds emigrated here during the period when Hungary ruled the principality. He said they were escaping persecution. The shepherds brought their customs and the names of their villages with them along with their sheep. It has become a tradition for villages which share kinship on both sides of the mountains to get together for an annual party.

In Baia de Arama, to the west of Târgu Jiu and in another county called Mehedinți, I meet Mariana Dăscălescu. She is a former mining engineer who has just started a women's weaving cooperative. Mariana is I guess in her late thirties, and she is determined to make her initiative a success. In a bare upstairs room of an otherwise empty building, six women have made a gorgeous Oltenian-style carpet on a giant loom. The carpet measures about eight foot by six foot and has a bright red central field with a wide, dark blue border. Characteristically, in field and border there are white, pink, blue and yellow flowers of different varieties on stems; they look as though a child has placed each one separately and at equal distances with great care in preparation for a game. The weavers have come to Mariana because they are out of work or have to spend a lot of time at home to look after dependents. She has paid for their training; she also buys the wool for them and has borrowed money to set up more looms. The Mayor of Baia de Arama has given the cooperative a workshop which is being completed when I arrive. The bare building is just a temporary home. To help the women sell their work more widely, Mariana has a shop in Bucharest and in Turnu Severin, the ancient Roman town on the Danube where she lives.

On the way back to Târgu Jiu, Ion the driver points out an 18th century 'cula'. This is a three-storey fortified manor house built to withstand sieges; it is one of several in Oltenia and shaped like a cube with a pitched roof on top. Although not the most beautiful I have seen, it is rugged and unpretentious. Opposite is the workshop of one of Gorj's few remaining dynastic potters: the work he does is like the 'cule': rugged and unpretentious. We take a short cut and pass through a concrete and asphalt desert. It is a 1950s town that provides homes for mining families. Everything about it looks hard

and buff-coloured. The only soft thing is the people. The road from here to Târgu Jiu is lined with slag heaps that have smothered a river valley. I look at them hoping for some prettifying factor; there is none. They are just there. Ion tells me horror stories about flooded salt workings which have undermined hundreds of houses. Shaking his wise, middle-aged head he says:

"Bad planning, short-term thinking - they never pay."

He would get on a treat with London cabbies.

Crossing the line: north into Transylvania

The companionable Ion gives me a lift to Alba Iulia, another act of kindness for which I owe thanks to the director of Gorj's cultural inspectorate. On the way we drive north through the spectacular Jiu Defile and into Transylvania. Ion and I try a conversation about

Romanian politics; from my point of view he is frustratingly conventional and will not be drawn into making dangerous admissions. From his point of view I am probably asking too many questions; he is a diplomat and a survivor by nature and in any case, he needs to keep his eyes on the road.

We enter the Jiu Valley, through the mining town of Petroşani. Although grimly functional, Petroşani has an odd sort of attraction owing to the fact that the town has been laid out with an eye for symmetry; it is uncluttered too, and someone somewhere has made the grand decision that pitched roofs were more practical than flat ones, so the roofscape is much less uncompromising than it might have been. Its hard-bitten appearance is softened by the mountains and valleys which encircle it. Mining has been a way of life in these mountains for thousands of years. But given the image which I already had of the area, I was surprised to find myself liking Petroşani.

Sarmizegetusa

Petroşani lies 50 kilometres to the south of the citadel of Sarmizegetusa, the barely accessible royal fortress which the Iron Age Dacians built in the Southern Carpathians more than two thousand years ago. It was much more than a citadel: Sarmizegetusa was the Dacians' capital and a self-contained, self-supporting community comprising craftsmen, astronomers, and farmers who systematically husbanded cattle, pigs and sheep. As well as managing the forests and constructing sophisticated stone walls, the Dacians mined iron from the mountains.

It is still more or less a secret place and you cannot reach it without a four-wheel drive. The excavations that have been done leave many questions unanswered: no-one even knows the full extent of the site. But Sarmizegetusa is more real than Camelot, and King Decebal of the Dacians is less of a myth than Arthur. Sarmizegetusa was where Decebal made his last stand before swallowing poison to avoid capture by the Romans.

Sarmizegetusa and the Dacians are a part of the fabric of Romanian myths of origin. The myths started to take political shape in the late 18th century and they survived into the communist period. According to these myths the Dacians presided over a golden era, as did Stephen the Great in Moldavia, and Constantin Brâncoveanu in Wallachia. People hark back to the Roman occupation too. Romanian is a Latin language, and the Vlachs who populated the lower Danube after the legions left Dacia were considered well-educated heirs to Roman civilisation. Since the 1989 revolution some young historians have tried to debunk the myths of origin. They see them as a dangerous illusion that can damage the country's efforts to reform. I am all for Romanians getting real about themselves, but I hanker for a sense of history and identity. If you destroy them, what is left is not worth having. Brooding on irreconcilable opposites and the general destructiveness of the human race, I stay silent, looking for signs of hope in the landscape.

Further on the road cuts between parcels of derelict farmland.

"This area used to be covered with fruit trees," says Ion. "After the Revolution the țărani cut them all down and sold them for wood. Now the land is sterile and useless – where's the sense?" Ion shakes his head, unable to find words for the stupidity of such an act.

We stop to eat in a café used mainly by truck drivers. Besides the manageress, I am the only woman. There is no tension though; probably nobody notices I am there except me. The air inside the café is thick with cigarette smoke, but the plate of liver, bacon and fried potatoes which the manageress brings in five minutes flat tastes fabulous. Ion does not eat anything; he has a lemon juice and buys another packet of Carpați smokes. It is getting dark by the time we reach Alba; Ion drives me meticulously into the citadel. Having delivered me safely to the porticoed entrance of Muzeul al Unirii, he faces a three-hour return journey. A thousand years later I wonder if I should have given him a tip.

Part IV

The Apuseni

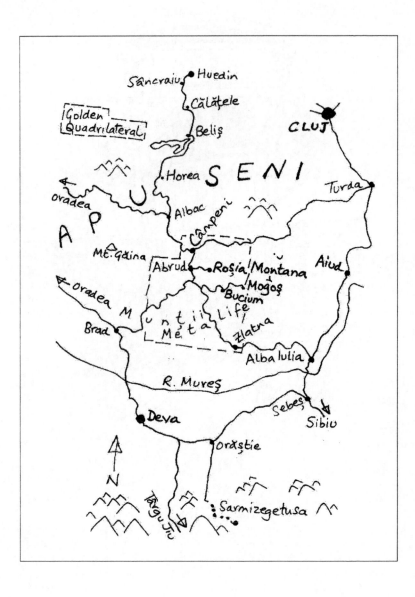

On the map they are a splatter that spoils the Carpathians' curve. The Apuseni Mountains are technically part of the Southern Carpathians, but they have an independent identity. Their name is a lyrical word for the West; in my interpretation it means 'the place where the sun sets', or 'the mountains that lie down with the sun'. The Apuseni separate Transylvania geographically from the Banat and the Great Hungarian Plain. They consist of many smaller ranges that intersect each other haphazardly from all sides of the compass. At their southern end, the Mureş River cuts between them and the main Carpathian ranges. To the north, the Apuseni fall short of the Eastern Carpathians leaving a wide corridor for the Someş River and Ţara Codrului, The Wooded Land.

A cradle of rock

Nor does their greatest impact come from their height. The Apuseni are not nearly as tall as the biggest Carpathians and few of the peaks rise over 1800 metres. They are mere molehills when compared with the Alps. If Romanians speak about them in nostalgic tones, they do so because these mountains are the legendary cradle of Dacian civilisation. The Apuseni have yielded some of Europe's most exciting archaeological discoveries, and they are home to the oldest rural communities in Romania. These are not their only treasures: in the areas unspoilt by industrialisation – and there are lots of them - the mountains and valleys are strikingly beautiful. They are a geologist's dream: deposits of marble, outcrops of snow-white limestone, giant basalt crags and karsts like enormous sea sponges with spectacular caves. In the caves archaeologists have found proof of a prehistoric bear cult.

The Golden Quadrilateral

The Apuseni contain gold, silver, copper and uranium. Precious metals have been exploited here for at least four thousand years. The gold mines, both ancient and modern, lie within an odd-shaped area in the central Apuseni which people call The Golden Quadrilateral. Across the quadrilateral stretches a mountain range called Munţii Metaliferi, the Metal-Bearing Mountains.

    The Apuseni's gold has made them the target of all kinds of attention, some welcome, some not. One of the main reasons that the Romans invaded Dacia was to get hold of their huge gold deposits. From 106 to 273 AD, the Romans mined most of their gold in

133

Transylvania. In 131, the Romans founded Alburnus Major. In effect the town was the Empire's bank, employing hundreds of miners on short-term contracts. The workers came from all over the Roman sphere of influence, but most of them were Dalmatians, from present-day Croatia and Bosnia. Alburnus Major spread across the narrow valley and over several hillsides, leaving signs of its prosperity in the roads, administrative buildings, workshops, houses, mausolea and miles of extraordinary galleries which are beginning to come to light. The site has only just started to be excavated in its entirety. When the Romans left, others stepped into their shoes. Gold has always had a double-edged character, part blessing, part curse. As I was to find out later the conflict between the two is as powerful today as it ever was.

Greenhorns in the Gilău Mountains

I first went to the Apuseni in 1995. Kit and I were driving a white Corsa which he had hired in Budapest. It was getting dark and our nerves were starting to crackle and snap. We did not know where we were going except that it was north. I was sulking, resenting his universal competence, wanting Romania to myself without intrusions. To make matters worse, I had not eaten for three hours; I need to nosh at regular intervals or I become a fiend. Kit had to catch a plane home in two days time; we only had a few hours to explore the Apuseni.

We (or rather Kit) chose the road from Albac to Huedin; on the map it looked large and confident. It looked like a journey of 80 or 90 kms, and should have been easy for a couple of experienced travellers like ourselves.

The relatively broad white ribbon on the map turned out to be a cart track with an occasional few metres of concrete sets to keep your spirits up. We were driving in the twilight along a road with no markings. Valleys came and went in the gloaming along with forests and clearings. There was absolutely no other traffic whatever, not even a cart. We kept taking wrong turnings; there were no sign posts and we had to rely on Kit's expertise as a rally driver's navigator to find our way. The car's 900 hp engine whined complainingly as Kit tried to nurse it over lumps of hardened dung, potholes and gaping craters that opened before us without the courtesy of a warning. I sniped impatiently, wanting more time to look. We were always rushing everywhere.

"I'm tired; can't we stop?"

"If we stop, we won't find anywhere to eat and we won't be able to sleep."

"But I'm exhausted and you don't know where we're going; maybe there won't be anywhere to stay. I'd rather stay here and sleep in the car. Or even outside." The soft trees and wispy grasses looked so inviting.

"There might be bears; anyhow I've got to get home - and you're supposed to be the expert on this country, not me."

"Haven't you got any biscuits?" I whined, surprised and ashamed of myself at the same time.

"No, I gave you my last one hours ago."

I felt like crying.

On the point of calling the whole thing off - except that the further we went, the less possible this became - we found a new inn beside a man-made lake called Fântenele. In our room was a dismantled public address system and unidentifiable wires connected to plugs between the beds. Kit bounced up and down on the hard mattresses, infuriatingly cheerful:

"Look - they're going listen to us! Let's give them some real fun."

A hunting party was eating in the restaurant; they were all men, heartily toasting each other with bubbly while pretty waitresses attended to their every whim. Kit and I sat waiting in savage silence. Cold, tired and still hungry, having devoured the last bread stick, we would have eaten each other given half a chance.

In the morning, refreshed by cold coffee, stale bread and an omelette 'fără nimic' (an empty omelette, 'au naturel'), we find Beliş, a village that had been shifted wholesale from the valley floor to make way for the lake. Its wooden church had been moved as well. As a settlement it looked distinctly unnatural, just plonked on the hillside. The church was lovely, with an arcaded porch at its west end.

Winding down the mountain side to Huedin, we passed ten Roma women and a man. They had spread out across the road. The women looked happy and beautiful in their swirly red and green skirts; the man wore a shifty expression.

"Go on, take the chance! Get a photo!" Kit pulled the Corsa over and I got out, eager to catch them but worried about their reactions. There was no embarrassment on the other side: the Roma clustered around me and I saw that one of the women had a baby in her arms. It was wrapped in swaddling clothes. I took several snaps and by the time I had finished even the man was smiling. For a moment our guard was down.

Alina the ethnographer in Bucharest had told me the Apuseni contained the roots of Romania's indigenous culture, in so far as they could be traced. She was not the only expert to mention them. I knew they were stiff with legends and folklore and I was hoping to find the mountains a haven of undisturbed antiquity. Of course this was foolish: they had been disturbed many times and the antiquity was evaporating. But the richness of Romania's traditions still amazed me and I wanted to look closer. I had seen convoys of Moți on their way to Timişoara in covered carts. At first I had thought they were Roma. Several years went by before I had a chance to return. My first real contact with Apuseni people came when I went to Bucium.

A picture of Bucium

The 'comuna' of Bucium consists of six villages, each one nestling in its own valley. There are Bucium Sat, Bucium Şasa, Cerbu, Izbita, Muntarii and Bucium Poieni. Bucium lies within the Golden Quadrilateral, to the south of Roşia Montana. Its name comes from the Latin for 'alphorn'. Old people living on the farms say they remember 'buciumi' being made here. But not any more. Nowadays shepherds who want to contact each other from the opposite sides of a valley have to rely on yelling.

Bucium Poieni means Bucium on the Meadow; its nearest neighbour is Bucium Şasa, Bucium on the Riverbank. If you clamber to the top of one of the hills that shoots up from the main street of Bucium Poieni, and walk up through the beech woods for twenty minutes you emerge on a ridge. From there you can look out over a wonderful panorama that reaches from Roşia Montana to the northwest and south to the flat-topped peak of Vulcan. Below you are the wooded valleys of Corna, Văleni and Şasa. All of these are due to be demolished.

Bucium Poieni is the largest village in the comuna, and most people refer to it simply as Bucium. Its main street stretches for about three miles from end to end. At the bottom end, the one nearest the turn-off from the road to Valea Alba, it is in quite good repair, and even has a bit of tarmac on it. On either side of the street is a single, fragmented row of houses made of timber, or brick or concrete. Wood predominates, but shortly after you start the uphill climb you pass a funny little two-storey concrete block with a flat roof. It arrived there against every natural law of planning when times were hard: concrete is always cheaper than stone. It is incredibly ugly, but it has a garden full of chrysanthemums, cosmos and cabbages and this takes the edge off its awfulness. The timber houses are mounted on a ground floor of rounded river stones. All the houses have gardens; some of them are farms with substantial steadings. A stream runs parallel to the street. Every so often a bridge crosses it, or it becomes a ford, and there are horrible tangles of rubbish caught up in the bank. Someone has left a large wooden washing tub in the water and occasionally you find a gem: a chair with nicely turned legs or a trap for catching ferrets.

A few hundred metres from the turning, there is a derelict two-storey L-shaped house covered in lime plaster the colour of ochre. It must have been a magnificent creature: wide and spacious, and splendidly adorned with a wide balcony facing into an inner courtyard, while a carriage entrance punctuates the ground-floor façade. A gaggle of tall, narrow, ugly brick chimneys sticks out of its roof, spoiling the silhouette. On enquiry I discovered the house had belonged to a wealthy priest who lived here in Bucium's heyday; then it became a secondary school and was now empty. A few more gusts of wind would make the roof cave in. A couple of fat cows were grazing on what might have been the vicarage lawn.

About half-way up, Bucium's main street widens into a square of sorts; it is more of an irregular rectangle that vaguely interrupts the thoroughfare. It has none of the civic importance that a village square might be expected to have, or rather that I suddenly, unreasonably want it to have. Bucium is struggling against dereliction. To one side there is a church and village hall, and a building that contains the parish house on its first floor and someone else's home and a shop beneath; all the windows have plain wooden shutters. Opposite, across the stream, is a working forge. On the third side is a handsome, two-storey building with well-proportioned windows framed in stucco relief. It has a plaster façade and is being done up from head to toe with grey paint. On the last side is a private garden but its fence is so tall I cannot see behind it. The square is paved with cobbles and, as my bourgeois expectations dilate with the sheer fatigue of carrying them, I realise that it is wide enough for a village hop. Bucium welcomes the free of spirit.

Going down the road one morning to fetch bread I see a Roma man mending a flue pipe on a trestle table under a makeshift shelter. He has to be a gypsy with a dark face and clothes like that; you can sense it instantly, however reluctant you are to show prejudice. His name is Mihai and he is from Târgu Mureş, a city on the Transylvanian plateau. Târgu Mureş has a strongly Hungarian identity and as well as Romanian and the Roma tongue, Mihai speaks fluent Magyarul. His eyes are excessively bright, and full of mischief, like a naughty child's. He tries to sell me some 'antique' furniture and, because of his unbelievable pleading, quick-fire tongue and inoffensive cheek, nearly succeeds.

Actually, in a fit of excitement that comes from being a potential home-owner in Bucium, I buy an iron-work window grille for $20. It is handsome without being museum material; when I ask Mihai where it came from he looks evasive:

"I found it somewhere!"

It is OK, I tell him, I am not accusing him of stealing, just interested in architectural history. The grille's spikes are bent and I take it to the forge for straightening. The blacksmith drops what he is doing and hammers them flat. There is a learned discussion among onlookers as to whether this is the best method: maybe he should have fired them first. The blacksmith ignores these backseat drivers, and in five minutes hands me back the grille with a satisfied grunt. I offer him money; he sweeps it aside with a lordly gesture.

"Buy me a beer sometime," he says. I begin to understand why Buciumani have a reputation for grandeur. To call these people peasants would be absurd. Mihai sidles up to me, his eyes sparkling with hilarity:

"I have another one just like it at home; don't you want to buy that one too?"

Behind the row of houses along the main street the land climbs precipitously on either side, and it seems that any animals grazing there must have longer legs at the back than the front. There are one or two cows in each pasture, a straggle of sheep and horses, some grazing free, some hobbled. Where the valley sides open out, you can see into other valleys; the dovetailing network continues apparently for ever. It is a scene of wonderful greenness; there are a few ploughed fields, isolated behind wooden fences. From a distance, most of the landscape is velvet-smooth pasture, dotted with trees and haystacks with attitude.

The further you go, the more rudimentary Bucium's main street becomes, until it peters out into a muddy footpath in a ditch between two high banks of red soil. Keep on to the top and you reach a forest backroad, designed for carts and used by trucks ferrying logs or stone. The forest roads have only been there since the 1960s; before that locals knew the ways but foreigners would often get lost. Up there, you can see across the veined complexity of the Apuseni. Early in the morning, when the mist lies heavy in the valleys, the ridges stand out starkly, giving an impression of permanence that is reassuring and, sadly, false.

One day while wandering up a hillside, I met an elderly couple coming down from their hill-top field where they grew potatoes.

"Where have you come from?" the woman asked.

"From Wales," I said. "The Land of the Vlachs."

"Ah," they said, and if they were mystified, they did not show it. "And what are you doing here?"

138

"Just enjoying the view. And trying to help save Roşia Montana. What do you think about the mine?"

"We are not going to move," declared the woman. "We were born here and here we will die! Do you like our country?"

"It is unbelievably lovely," I say, and turn towards the huge hazel trees whose branches have spread so wide and low over the ground that you can hardly get underneath them.

Nicoleta is twenty-five. She runs a combined shop, post-office, bar and telephone service which is more of a focal point for the village than the church. Nicoleta teaches French at the local infant school. She is slightly built and pretty with light brown hair and a dazzling, trustworthy smile; she has quick movements and a quick brain and, as befits a farmer's daughter, her sense of humour is earthy. You cannot shock Nicoleta. She realises that I am having trouble with the local accent and is instantly ready to interpret for me and explain what is going on.

Nicoleta's husband Ovidiu is also in his twenties; he works in the copper quarry at Roşia Poieni, not far from Roşia Montana. It is dirty, back-breaking work, he says; many men have developed respiratory problems from the filthy atmosphere. Ovidiu is tall, athletic, good-looking and has a ready, open smile with a hint of anxiety in it. He and Nicoleta were married three years ago; it was the traditional affair with two ceremonies and a three-day party. Now they are expecting their first child.

Ovidiu is interested in local history and has started collecting old objects that no-one else wants: sepia photographs, letters, woodwork and clothes. At the moment he stores them in boxes in his garage. He knows the local legends, some of which are half true: Fefeleaga, the woman from Bucium Şasa with a very thin horse. She had nothing left but stones because the foreigners had taken all the gold. Her horse symbolised the village's abject poverty. Fefeleaga's house is still there, an abject ruin.

"My grandmother told me there are Roman mines in Bucium; she said they have extraordinary, rectangular galleries that had been excavated one beneath the other. I don't know if it's true. Nobody knows. Maybe we will have a look for them when you come back again!" I nod enthusiastically, hardly able to believe my ears.

Nicoleta and Ovidiu live in part of her parents' house which is separated into two buildings, one for sleeping in, the other for eating and storing food, on either side of a steeply sloping courtyard. At the top end of the yard is a long, rough trestle table and a bench behind it. In good weather, and sometimes in bad, this acts as the bar.

Nicoleta's father, Petru, is a Moţ in his early fifties, a round-faced, jovial, comfortable, portly man who loves a joke. His ruddy cheeks come not only from his outdoor lifestyle but from high blood pressure; he has to be careful of his heart. Petru is still more than capable of running a few head of cattle on the family's land. And, as long as the sick cow he is worried about gets better, he graciously consents to drive me to Mogoş in his cart on the following day.

By cart to Mogoş

There was no cart trip in the morning. In the event the cow took a turn for the worse; she had a still-born calf inside her and could not stand up. It was a minor tragedy for Petru and his family: they could not decide whether to send for the vet, who lived an hour's drive away in Câmpeni. His fee would be a phenomenal amount for them. The other option was to have the animal put down. If they chose the former, there would be no guarantee that their cow would improve, and they would lose their money; if the latter, the butcher might refuse to take the carcass on the grounds that the cow was diseased. When I went to see them, Nicoleta and Viorica were frantic, and Viorica was on the verge of tears. Petru barely spoke to me.

Next morning, however, a message arrives that all is well; I can go to Mogoş. The cow died and the butcher agreed to take her away. Everyone is smiling, except the cow.

Nicoleta's father has a fine roan horse called Şoimu (Falcon). He is a stocky, sturdy seven year old stallion. He is built like a Welsh cob. I had hired them both for the day so that I could enjoy the pleasure of being driven to Mogoş, a village fourteen kilometres away in a neighbouring valley, and back. There was no particular reason for going, except that it was there, and feasible in a day. An English woman once travelled through Transylvania in an ox-cart. Her book about the journey had made her literary reputation. She was called Mrs Lion Phillimore and must have been a tough bird, because Romanian farmers' carts are not built for luxury travel. Lion Phillimore lived in the days when all doors opened to the daughters of the British Empire. Maybe there was a vestige of that hope left in me – in any case I liked her eccentricity. But I did not fancy an ox-cart half so much as one pulled by Şoimu.

Petru had dressed for the occasion in a black leather jacket and a porkpie hat with a kingfisher's feather in it. After harnessing the horse, he ushered me into the back of the cart where he had thoughtfully placed a bundle of hay covered with a tarpaulin for me to sit on. The hay was for Şoimu's lunch. I had brought a macin-

tosh in case the heavens opened. The V-shaped vehicle swung from side to side as we set off. Eventually, lodged in a half-crouching, half-sitting position I settled back to enjoy the sensation. It was a bit like riding in a wooden bath, not because it was wet but because of the amazed grins on the faces of passers-by. I felt socially exposed, the eccentric's curse. Nobody chooses to travel by cart when they can go by car, not in early 21st century Romania at any rate.

We followed the pitted asphalt road beside the Alba River and then climbed through luxuriant forests of hazel, beech, ash and hornbeam. Above the woods the road faded away and became a forest track of red earth. A green and beige landscape contained by an ominous-looking mist hedged us in; little box trees grew wild in the meadows and the air was tangy with the advancing autumn.

A Roma boy hailed us from the roadside, then stared with furious intensity as we passed him by. We had crested the pass and Șoimu was pounding downhill. The world which had been green to my heart's content in Bucium miraculously became greener. On the opposite hillside was a building of astonishing dimensions: its roof was four times the height of its walls. It appeared to be thatched. We turned a corner and there was another one below us, much nearer. Such an object demanded a closer look. Petru obligingly pulled over and put the brake on so that I could study this weird phenomenon. The building perched on a small piece of flat ground in a plunging meadow. It had a wooden fence around it and a retinue of haystacks. I found a gap in the wire fence, and ran down the hill to see if my eyes had tricked me. There it was, a thatched animal barn of a kind I had seen in the Cluj village museum. It was called a 'șura' and is a speciality of the Apuseni. The walls are made of timber and soft grass is pushed into the roof slats freestyle, resulting in a look that reminded me of haystacks rather than English country cottages. When the thatch gets old, bits of it fall off leaving the impression of moth-eaten buffalo hide. The height of the roofs is entirely practical; snow slides off them easily. Petru had gamely followed me, and by the time I had inspected all four sides of the șura he was sitting having a chat with the old woman who had emerged from the inside carrying a wooden pitch fork. I took pictures of them side by side on the bench outside the door: the proprietress looked suitably reticent in the company of a total stranger, but Petru was grinning fit to bust.

On the way back up to the road, he was puffing like a steam train and his face was puce. He thumped his chest on the left hand side:

"Inima!" he said between pants, "...my heart!" I tried to calm him down and make him promise that he would not overdo it; otherwise, I said, we would return immediately. Petru waved these protestations aside: no, he would not hear of it. I hoped it was because he was enjoying the jaunt and not just the chance to earn some extra cash. After the first close sighting of a şura, they came thick and fast, by themselves or in conversational groups.

It started to rain on the way down to Mogoş, but the landscape was idyllic. There was no sound of quarrying, but when we arrived in the valley bottom and disembarked in Mogoş's main square, I saw a bulldozer making orange gashes in the green meadow on the opposite hillside. Petru had gone into the village shop to buy cigarettes. When he came out, I asked him what was going on.

"I don't know," he said, then asked a man who was leaning against the shop doorway.

"Oh it's just some people who live on the hill making a new roadway," he answered, "Don't worry, it's nothing to do with a mine!"

Mogoş is the name of a comuna, and this district, smaller than Bucium, has the look of a long-forgotten place. Most of the village houses seem to have seen better days, but someone has built a spanking new café in the square. It has pantiles, bright white walls and angular windows. I walk up a side road and come across a farm-yard complete with şura, haystacks and three women who are unloading hay from the stacks and tossing it into the barn.

As I prepare to take a photo, two men arrive leading a pair of oxen with a cart attached. The oxen are yoked together with a piece of shaped and polished wood decorated with noughts and crosses. I photograph the entire group, oxen and all.

"What do you think of our village," asks a woman.

"Great," I tell her. "What potential for sustainable development you have here!" She looks at me sceptically; a lot of stupid tourists probably say that. But it is true. Not that tourism alone is the answer to rural Romania's problems, but a sensitively managed eco-system of small businesses that could sustain the local population and provide its food without destroying the environment, that could be an answer and include tourism too. My image of an acceptable, non-invasive holiday trade does not tally with that of the

142

government departments and companies who decide such things: the men in suits see only the large-capacity hotels, casinos, vast marinas and glitz that would obliterate the local economy and ways of life. They would probably plant palm trees in Valea Alba.

Feeling depressed, I walk back to the cart; who the hell am I to tell these people how to live? Next to the cart a detached and hobbled Şoimu is enjoying a leisurely munch. Petru has thrown a blanket over his back to keep him warm; it is still drizzling and visibility is down to a few hundred yards. Petru is exchanging gossip and worldly wisdom with a couple who are loading heavy jute sacks and woollen bags onto a pony. The pony is a three-year old mare with a bright eye and fine legs; she is also remarkably calm as her owners lash the bags onto the pack saddle. This has a timber frame which follows the contours of a conventional saddle tree; just like the one in the stâna above Şurdeşti it looks extremely uncomfortable to sit on.

Petru knows I am making notes and tells me informatively that the pack saddle is called a 'tarniţă'. This is another photo opportunity; who knows for how much longer the villagers of Mogoş will walk to market with their pack ponies? The woman holding the mare says to me,

"Hey, why don't you visit us? We only live a few miles over the hill. Oh, you are leaving soon? Never mind, take my address, and next time you come, be sure to knock on our door. Everyone knows where we live." She writes her name and address in my notebook. Her name is Valeria, her address simply Mogoş-Negreşti, with no house name or number or street. Valeria looks like a woman of sensitivity and good sense. It would not be impossible to explain how much I would like her to preserve her way of life without forcing her to stay poor. However, given the differences in our circumstances I decide that to do so now would be tactless in the extreme.

I still have the notes I made; they are just fragments, to be expanded at some future date.

We press on for three kilometres along a rutted road beside the valley bottom to a village called Bârleşti. I sit huddled in the back of the cart, and my eyes soak in details of barns and farm implements, stacks of freshly sawn timber cut neatly to exact lengths, the shapes of fields and woodlands, the unobtrusiveness of rural life. Because of the weather the landscape now seems morose. One or two lorries thunder past us, sending up colossal sprays from lake-sized puddles. It is getting late; we decide to turn for home. Feeling more like Queen Victoria on a bad day than Lion Phillimore, I sink into the wet remains of Şoimu's hay and think not of England, but of how to change the hearts and minds of those in power.

Petru brings us safely home by four o'clock. Even in the rain he has been cheerful, but becomes noticeably more so when we reach the house with a sign announcing 'Coiffure Angelini', the first human habitation you come to on entering Bucium Poieni from the east. I offer to help dry the horse and put him away, but Petru insists I go straight to his house. There, in the tiny, dark shed of a kitchen on a blazing woodburning cooker, Viorica is frying lamb chops with lashings of potato. Food makes everything look better. On the table are vast glass jars containing pickled peppers. I am so frozen that I try to climb into the cooker, and then notice two old people who are sitting beside the door. They are as rigid as icebergs.

"These are our cousins from Reghin," Viorica says. We exchange understanding smiles, "they have come to stay with us; they took the bus, poor things!" Judging by their appearance it was one of the old, unheated cross-country buses, not the new long-distance coaches that have made travelling on Romania's roads very nearly a pleasure. Viorica melts any residual chill in the atmosphere by handing round tots of savage, cherry-flavoured țuica; it is the one and only time that I have welcomed it. The next time I think about it, I have downed five glasses.

Nicoleta arrives and takes a seat, enjoying a few minutes of relaxation. We talk about the cow.

"It's the government's fault. They do nothing for us. We have to pay taxes for this and taxes for that; everything is getting so expensive. There are no subsidies like you have... Farming is becoming impossible!" Word for word, I have heard the same complaints back at home in Wales. I bleat something about self-reliance, knowing it sounds ridiculous. I am a late arrival on the green politics scene, and in any case, ideas about self-sufficiency have a long way to go in the UK, let alone Romania.

Petru and Ovidiu arrive soon afterwards and, once we have finished eating, I ask Ovidiu to tell me more about local mining history.

I picked up fragments from his narrative.

"Gold used to be regarded as a curse," he told me. "This attitude was particularly strong in the 19th century, and specially around the time of the French exploitation. It was the middlemen, the bright guys we called 'smecheri' - the businesspeople - who caused that. And the revolt was against them rather than the French... You'll see a lot of wayside crosses in the mountains; they are often dedicated to miners. There's one I know well, it says 'Noroc la Băişag' ('Good luck to the miners') - the old people use the word baia for mine in our language... Bucium has a lot of gold; there were five or six mines here until 1965 when the work stopped... Back in the 19th century, seventy percent of Buciumani had their own 'șteampuri' (the water-powered stone breaking mills). They used to take their gold to the exchange in Brad; it was held every six months. They bought food with it: potatoes or grain. In the meantime they would hide the gold in their shoes or in their houses somewhere..." Brad is a town to the west of the Apuseni on the main road between Oradea and Deva. It has a superb little museum dedicated to the history of gold mining. "You could say that the Buciumani are descended from the Dacians..." Ovidiu looked torn between pride and unwillingness to perjure himself. "They say that the Dacians hid their gold and silver in the network of caves and galleries in Negrileasa."

A walk to Detunata

Eugen is the Orthodox priest of Bucium Poieni. He is in his twenties and married with two gorgeous bouncy children aged around three and five years old. His wife works in the picturesque old chemist's shop in Abrud which I mentioned in the guide. Eugen comes from Târgu Mureș and finds Bucium a challenge.

"When I started here, people hardly ever came to church - I think there were maybe ten or eleven in the congregation at the main weekly service. Now there are perhaps forty or forty-five." I congratulate him, and he turns modestly away. Eugen has written a local history and, in the absence of a village museum, has made collections of local pottery, and of the attractive table and wall crosses that people have thrown out of their homes, preferring plastic flowers in cut glass vases. He has put the crosses up on the walls of his own house; each one is less than six inches tall, and has an elaborately curlicued wooden frame around the crucifix, as if restating the connection between Christianity and the Tree of Life. He found some icons painted on tin; someone had chucked them onto the rubbish dump at the back of the graveyard. They are not great works of art, but have an honest, childlike appeal. Eugen has cleaned them and put them up on his verandah.

Today when I visit, he is in overalls, helping to repoint and repaint the outside of his house. When I say I am interested in walking, he perks up visibly and volunteers to be my guide. Touching one knee, he says,

"As long as we don't go too fast – I had an injury a few months ago and have to be careful." I cannot imagine outpacing Eugen. "Let me make sure no-one needs me, and we can go."

Two hours later we meet again outside his house; he is wearing a tracksuit and trainers with a small haversack slung over his shoulders, every inch the keen mountaineer.

Detunata is one of two unusual basalt outcrops which are famous as local beauty spots. Its name comes from the fact that pieces of the vertical rock occasionally fall and come crashing down with such a bang that it sounds like a bomb going off. To get there from Bucium Poieni means a hike of about an hour and a half. It is already early afternoon and the days are starting to draw in. We must not dawdle. Eugen shows me the way through the muddy back streets, across the Alba river and up like a monkey - I have to use my hands to steady myself - climbing the springy hillside pastures that are fringed with bright yellow and lime green ash, aspen, cherry, birch and hazel trees with shots of amber beech and red sumac and prunus leaves. The berries are out in force, but the autumn colours are racing through: they have arrived and are on the way out again within a matter of eight or nine days. Breathless, I reach a narrow horizontal path and look back down on Bucium. It has the sun on its back and is a picture of contentment and loveliness.

Higher still we go, making our way through closer forest, following paths used by shepherds and cowherds, and people riding pack horses to get to their summer pastures. Today we are alone save for a flock of sheep that is circumnavigating a lonely homestead on a rise above us. Eugen speaks shyly of the fate that may lie in store for Bucium.

"If the mine comes, we will move of course," he admits reluctantly. "We have bought another house as a holiday home just in case."

Detunata towers over the surrounding landscape like an accusing finger. It is a mountain of vertical grey slivers stuck together like square pieces of pencil lead or a giant Cadbury's flake. At the top there are trees bravely waving in the breeze; at the bottom is a scree of fallen basalt chips, great boulders of rectangular rock growing pink and yellow lichens that glow in the afternoon sun.

"Coming up?" Eugen turns to me with a grin. I hesitate for a split second then follow him across the scree, trying not to turn my ankles in the deep gaps, hands and feet grasping the rock and roots. Eugen makes a wrong turning and I have to climb down, not liking heights but amazed at the fun I am having. Twisting around saplings, keeping my balance I watch the ground fall farther below us. Wet earth and leaves form a mulch and we can grip with our toes. A last heave, hoist and shift and we are there, perching like a couple of crows on our pinnacles of rock and gazing down over the other side of Detunata, a drop of three hundred feet to the nearest field of earth. A panorama of mountains curves round us, blue in the distance, green, yellow and red closer to. Right in front of us, two or three miles away as the crow flies, are the edges of the sand-coloured quarries of Roşia Montana. The worst pits are hidden on the other side, but it is a shock all the same. They cannot be more than five miles away. A faint but persistent rumbling noise carries on the wind.

"That is their earth-moving equipment," says Eugen. "You can hear it every day now. We never could before. If the company bulldozes the Bucium valleys it will be unbearable."

I ask Eugen about his experiences as a boy in Mureş county. Was it hard growing up under communism?

"I can't say that," he replies. "No, it wasn't hard. We never lacked for anything; my parents were always good to us and, no... people often like to make out that it was terrible, but for me it wasn't so bad. I had a job in a factory before going into the Church. Everyone had a job; you weren't allowed not to have one. Now, it is much harder, not specially for me but for everyone."

I persisted:

"Does that mean you would like to go back to a communist system?"

He smiled:

"Oh, no; there have been changes for the better. For example, I can talk to you freely now; before it wouldn't have been possible. But it is very hard all the same." His experiences did not tally with those of my close friends: the sense of outrage at the repressive nature of Ceauşescu's regime had been so much more acute; the intellectual damage which he had done often seemed to outweigh the physical. And I knew that in cities such as Bucharest there had been terrible food and power shortages; then there had been the enforced pregnancies which created so many unwanted, uncared-for babies. But I could well believe that life in the cities had been harsher than in the countryside.

We talk of religion, a subject that is naturally dear to Eugen's heart. It is clear that he wants to believe in the Church as something that not only uplifts the spirit and provides love in greater capacities than humans are capable of, but that also contains universal and impartial justice. When he hears I am not married but living with a partner, he looks slightly worried. Gently but severely, he rebukes me.

"That is not good. You know we in the Orthodox Church do not agree with this way of living. If you are happy, you should marry; if not...." His voice trails away, letting me fill in his words for myself. Then, more reasonably: "It is different if you do not have children." And a few seconds later, he turns to me again, his tip-tilted nose quivering with the joke: "You can come to Bucium with your partner and we will arrange a wedding here; it will be inexpensive too!"

On the way back we walk through tall spruce woods that are dripping with moss and lichens. Eugen sees some brown mushrooms, and he is off, jumping over dead branches and wading through leaves, spying food for free. He returns with a pocketful and offers them to me.

"No," I tell him, "take them home for supper; you found them, you keep them". He beams. The way home brings us through Bucium Şasa, where the river is in spate. We take a short cut through someone's garden; the owner spies us through her window. Eugen waves and I nearly fall flat on my face in the mud.

"I don't understand why people don't eat fresh fruit," he tells me conversationally. "Why would you want to have oranges that are imported and weeks old when you can eat fresh berries from the trees?" His innocence staggers me.

"But no-one grows their own fruit in the UK anymore," I say. "We have all these supermarkets flying stuff in for us every day. Of course tomatoes don't taste like they used to..." Eugen is taking in every word, appalled.

"No," he states decisively, "I don't see how people could prefer that. Nothing is so good as a wild blackberry or a cherry that comes straight from the tree. You lose all the vitamins; it's not healthy," This is the land where fresh walnuts fall at your feet.

A few days later, I meet Eugen in the village square; he is in his overalls again, nothing like a priest.

"Have you heard? There is going to be a protest in Roşia again?"

"Yes, I'm going to miss it." I am frustrated, but another deadline is looming.

"Well, you must come back soon – and we'll organise your wedding!"

Waltzing with bears

Françoise is a Belgian Amazon of striking proportions and long, blonde hair. She has worked in Romania for a decade and has made it her home. In addition to owning half of a little villa in a leafy backstreet of Bucharest, she bought a house at the forest end of Bucium, which she renovated and extended to make a holiday cottage. Not content with that, she acquired another house which she has repaired and converted into a self-catering hotel for 'les amoureux de la nature, et des traditions'. Françoise has taken Bucium to her heart, and wrapped it in a bear hug of proprietorial care.

"I love the Buciumani," she told me as we made the six-hour journey there from the capital. "They are like little children, but they are also very, very clever."

I followed Françoise's Bucium career from the pages of Formula AS. The weekly magazine has been championing the anti-quarry protest and encouraging everyone by its outspoken style. Meeting Françoise in the flesh was like meeting Astérix and Obélix rolled into one. On the day of the first Greenpeace protest, she drove her 4x4 up and down the village street calling on people to join the gathering throng and go with her to Roşia Montana. Dissenters or fence-sitters were treated to a furious Gallic outburst; smoking one of her favourite slender cheroots, Françoise treated them to a withering tirade, which usually began and ended with the phrase "If you do not come with us, you are not a true Buciuman". While some people grinned and took it in good part, others remained stony-faced, or melted away as though they had not heard. I could see why. With waverers, a head-on confrontation was not the way to win them over. And yet I had to admire her. Françoise had invested a huge amount of time, love and money into her hotel, and only a wimp would have stood by and done nothing.

On the way back to Bucharest, Françoise told me how, in the early days at her Romanian job, she had demonstrated outside the Belgian Embassy in Bucharest because a driver had tried to frame her for an accident that was not her fault.

"It was something they did a lot in those days," she said, eyes flashing. "Not any more. By making a fuss, not only in Romania but in Brussels too, I helped put a stop to it, and I would do it again today."

Saving Roşia Montana

The race to extract the precious gold no matter what the social and environmental cost is tearing this beautiful, historic, already damaged area apart. If plans for the latest exploitation go ahead, one of Europe's most exciting archaeological sites will be lost forever, along with thousands of homes, hundreds of little farms, a superb environment and a way of living in harmony with nature that has its roots in the ancient past. A great deal of money is involved and the stakes against saving Roşia Montana have grown very high.

Frankie is an archaeologist from Alba Iulia, the county town of Alba, into whose administrative area most of the Apuseni Mountains fall. In 1996 he was a bright, young curator at the county history and archaeology museum, Muzeul al Unirii. Frankie is a specialist in mountain archaeology and has written books on the prehistory of the region from the Neolithic period to the Roman. At the museum, he was second in command and keen to grab the chance to make Alba better known in the outside world. I met him when I was researching the guide; to help me get to know the area, he settled me down in the library with a pocket-sized book on a village I had never heard of. It was called Roşia Montana.

Underneath the village and outlying farms of Roşia Montana, in the middle of the Golden Quadrilateral, lies Alburnus Major. The Dacians exploited gold there, and the town was the most important mining centre in Europe. The present-day village contains some four thousand people, including those who live in outlying farms; Alburnus Major extended over a much larger area. Claiming to have had more or less continuous settlement since Roman times, Roşia Montana calls itself the oldest Romanian town. The Moţi, or 'mountain people', who live here say their roots are four thousand years old.

For the duration of the Roman occupation, Alburnus Major provided the empire with at least half of its gold - Trajan extracted over two billion American dollars' worth in current values; it also

paid for an empire-wide tax reduction that lasted one year, and for the superb amphitheatre in Verona. Hair clips made of gold from the Apuseni Mountains have been found in a pharaoh's tomb. The Apuseni were a source of Mycenean gold as well. Before mines came into existence, people trapped gold by laying fleeces in the gold-bearing rivers; this practice gave rise to the image of the Golden Fleece in the legend of Jason and the Argonauts. In the rivers of the Apuseni men and women pan for gold to this day.

In the late 1700s some waxed tablets were found showing the contracts which had been agreed between the mine workers and the entrepreneurs who ran the Roman mines. Nothing like them had ever come to light before. By the 1860s some forty-five tablets had been unearthed from Roşia Montana, some of them from the Catalina-Monuleşti seam which lies right underneath the present-day village.

When the Romans left, there were eight hundred years about which everyone seems hazy. People I meet in the area assure me that the mines were used during this period. Then in around 1000 AD the Hungarians came and granted concessions to Saxon miners; after them the Habsburgs arrived, and each in their turn developed the area and took its gold. The Saxons, Hungarians and Habsburgs built handsome houses with beautiful Baroque-style window frames and medallions carved out of stucco. Some of the houses in Roşia Montana have carriage entrances; above these in one or two cases I see the miners' crossed hatchets. Apart from some brave exceptions, where villages have been built anew or extensively repaired, the houses look run down. But they have tremendous character and a little research shows that they all have names: Casa Hanzel (Hanzel House), Casa lui Petri (Petri's House), Casa lui Bobar Ioan or Kiss or David Francisc, and most ornate of all, the Casino.

For part of the 19th and early 20th century, local people won the right to mine some of the seams for themselves, although they had done so individually for centuries. When I read up on Roşia Montana's history, the notes I had made when talking to Ovidiu became clear: in 1886, a group of French mining entrepreneurs tried to exploit the gold near Bucium Poieni. They focussed on a seam called Mina la Domn (the Master's Mine) in the area called Valea lui Ştefan. The French did not realise, or else did not care, that the Buciumani were the wealthiest, canniest and most awkward villagers in the Apuseni. Buciumani, rich or poor, do not answer kindly to anyone taking an unfair advantage of them. The villagers rose up

ROȘIA MONTANA

in protest, and working at night the Buciumani removed the remains of the gold from Valea lui Ştefan. The French were sent packing, and the story is recorded in a poem called Versul Buciumanilor, the closest thing the village has to annals. There are thousands of shafts in the mountains today, and the flame of private enterprise has never fully been extinguished.

Communist rule brought nationalisation to the mines and Roşia Montana's gold was sent by train to the Ukraine, benefitting its country of origin hardly at all. In the 1970s Ceauşescu decided he needed gold fast and gave the go-ahead for the first open cast pit at Roşia. A huge and very spectacular mountain called Cetate (Citadel), so riddled with Roman and later mine-workings that it looked like a ruined castle, was bulldozed to allow this quick fix to take place. The state continued to take gold and silver from Roşia, but on a much reduced level. Wages for the three hundred or so miners still employed there were pitifully low.

The following year we went there together. By this time the director of Muzeul al Unirii had retired and Frankie was there in his place. He used the museum's Dacia; our driver was Marcel, a pale young man with sensitive eyes and drooping shoulders. On the way to Roşia Montana we stopped to look at the site of a Dacian settlement in the Ampoiţa Valley, next to a striking outcrop of snow-white limestone. Further up the road was Zlatna, one of the most polluted towns in Romania. It had once been the regional Roman headquarters. Now it was an advertisement for all that was bad with the communist system and its successor: a dead-looking scape of poisoned land, poisoned people looking out to chimneys that exude sulphurous fumes and mountainous slag heaps from the nearby copper mines. Nothing grows on them, except that here and there a scraggy tree has sunk its roots into the buff-coloured waste, more out of hope than experience.

Frankie asked Marcel to stop so he could drop off some papers. While we were waiting, Marcel turned his sad eyes to me: "What do you think of our country?" he asked. "Isn't it a hopeless place?"

"Not at all," I said, fed up with the Romanians' continuous defeatism which treated every problem as insurmountable. "You have to fight your way out of this..." - 'this' meaning the despair which shrouded everything in Zlatna and so many other places and situations in Romania at that time. I did not mean to encourage him to fight physically, but intellectually, with spirit and conviction. It was easier for me. I came from a culture where 'civil society' had been established long enough to expect certain standards as of right. Marcel did not.

"You think we can?" he said. "What religion are you?"

I bridled, never liking this question, nor losing control of an argument.

"I don't have one," I said. "Religion causes more problems than it solves. What are you?"

"Jehovah's Witness," replied Marcel.

We pulled off the road in Abrud, a town of thirteen thousand people. It is in decay, and lies at the foot of the mountain road to Roşia Montana. Mud-coloured slag heaps greet you here as well. We are in the Golden Quadrilateral, where gold once paid for everything, but Abrud, with its plethora of churches, its proud façades, its elegant balconies and caryatids, is breaking up before our eyes. Its roads are full of potholes and there is no fresh paint anywhere. Everything looks colourless. Frankie showed me the oldest chemists' shop in town; it has tall, wooden cabinets containing row upon row of little drawers labelled with the Latin names of plant extracts and chemicals in florid script. The Orthodox church in the town centre is supported by a row of shopping arcades on either side as it was in the 16th century.

The road from Abrud to Roşia Montana is five kilometres long. Today the journey brings you from a state of reasonable sanity to paranoia and suspicion. It was not like that the first time I went. It was just a peaceful backwater then, somewhere to include in the guide that might earn a few brownie points for extra diligence.

Frankie showed me the modest open air museum which some bright sparks from Roşia Montana had founded in the 1970s. It contained wonderfully complicated contraptions for processing gold and one of the last remaining wooden 'şteamp' (stamping mill) which pummelled gold-bearing rocks into pieces small enough to be sorted by hand. They were part of a revolution in semi-industrial water-powered machinery for which Romania can claim a central rôle. Every household in Roşia Montana and the other mining towns and villages of the Golden Quadrilateral had a şteamp until Ceauşescu issued an order for their destruction. Behind this last one was a row of Roman tombstones showing family groups. Some of the clothes they were wearing proved that the Romans and Dacians were not always bitter enemies.

There was no-one there but us. To one side of the museum in the side of a hill known as Orlea was the opening of a restored mine shaft complete with rails and a trolley. Beside it a door opened onto a steep stairway that led down into the only Roman gallery that had been fully excavated. Walls and roof of the gallery had been chiselled into precision-straightness and every few yards there was a niche containing lamp holders and the remains of iron tools.

Frankie said there were miles of such galleries waiting to be rediscovered. But there was no money available to do it.

We walked up the main street into the centre of Roșia Montana. On either side, there were houses of good proportions; some had Baroque-style stucco ornament, others were more Neo-Classical in feel. In the main square was a handsome façade of three storeys. It was *just* a façade; the rest of the building had collapsed. Trees were growing from the top of the walls. To the right a cobbled street led to the upper part of the village; it became narrower as we climbed. Set back from the lane was a pretty white-painted church falling into ruin; we walked past neat gardens and the road became stone track. Higher still we reached a stand of firs which sheltered some minute wooden chalets known as 'popașuri' (holiday cabins), and a few minutes further on we came out onto a meadow. To our right was Tăul Angelului (Angel Lake). It was one of hundreds of man-made lakes that peppered the gold-bearing regions of the Apuseni; tanks that fed the water-powered steampuri. From there we looked out over Roșia Montana and its neighbouring mountains and valleys. The view was stupendous. Far away to the south-west was the anvil shape of Vulcan. I did not notice that Cetate was not there. The existing quarry was out of sight. The open pits of Roșia Poieni did not impinge on my view at all.

Coming back down again we passed a wedding party loafing around in the lane. A fir tree decked with streamers stood on either side of an arched gateway. From an upstairs window a girl in pink chiffon was leaning out, swapping insults with a young man on the ground who had hair like James Dean. We crossed to the other side of upper Roșia Montana and clambered over a rock fall into the mouth of a medieval mine shaft. A lot of Roșia's gold lay near the surface. People had got it out by a method called 'fire and water' - heating the rocks until they were red hot and then pouring water on them to make them explode. Fragments of reddened, blackened, shattered stone lay all around us. Inside the cave several holes showed where the miners had bored their way into the gold seams. Their galleries were crude by comparison with the Roman ones.

Back in the centre of the village, a few Dacias came and went. An old woman belaboured a pair of oxen that were ambling forwards, pulling a cart as though time grew on trees.

Frankie's enthusiasm for Roșia Montana infected me. He was an honest, hard-working and dedicated man and these qualities shone through him. I could not guess what he earned but judging by most museum jobs at the time, it would be the equivalent of around 25 US dollars a month. He asked for nothing except an engagement of interest. In the following autumn he sent me a message: some prospectors had been working in Roșia Montana. They had been taking rock samples. He thought they were Australians. Frankie was worried; nobody had contacted him to ask his permission. He was afraid that the fragile archaeological and cultural eco-systems of Roşia Montana were about to come tumbling down.

By this time I am back home in the UK and preoccupied with other matters. Romania seems far away but a sense of urgency keeps nagging me. There is something different about this message; Frankie is the last person to ask for help unless it is absolutely vital. Like it or not, I am personally involved. Maybe it is time for the worm to turn.

The company is not Australian but a joint Canadian-Romanian venture with most of the profits - and other benefits – apparently going to the Canadian side. From the information that is available, and judging by past experience, I believe that the cost of exploitation will be unacceptably high in relation to what the Romanians, and especially the villagers of Roşia Montana and the other affected areas, will get in return. Many of the villagers share this opinion but their voices can barely be heard above the expensive propaganda campaign which the company is waging.

If what Frankie has told me is right, Roşia Montana could be one of the most exciting Roman discoveries in Europe. But it seems that everyone, except him, is playing it down. A team of French archaeologists, whom Frankie has enabled to dig in the area, starts negotiating with the company to save some of the site. The French team leader wants the company to pay for a new museum and visitor centre, and save the best of the Roman galleries as well. Otherwise, the entire, mostly unexplored area of Roşia Montana's Dacian, Roman, medieval, Hungarian and Habsburg mining heritage will be bulldozed. Some 700 homes and 140 apartments will be flattened. Around 2000 people will have to move. There are serious doubts hanging over the method of extraction. In the conditions we have here, the gold is too widely dispersed to be mined underground; it will have to be leached from the rock with cyanide. Many European countries have banned this technique on the grounds that it is too dangerous.

In 1997 the village of Bergama, near the ancient Greek site of Pergamon in western Turkey, persuades the government in Ankara to cancel a licence granted to a part-Australian mining company called Gold Digger. The villagers are terrified that a 900-litre cyanide pond will leak. The Canadian-Romanian company that aims to exploit the Apuseni region goes by the name of Goldigger. Squawks are heard coming from the company's Romanian office, but the executives of Goldigger swear there is no connection between the two. Not long afterwards the company changes its name. In December 1999, a delegation of villagers from Roşia Montana hands in a petition to the prefect in Alba Iulia. The petition expresses their concerns over the social, economic and environmental aspects of the mining project, and about the threat to the archaeology too.

The founder and Chief Executive of the company which is interested in taking the remains of the gold from the Apuseni is Romanian by birth. He fled the country in 1978 after his father died in a mining accident. Having made a fortune from undisclosed sources, he returned to Romania in 1996, and presented himself on television and in the newspapers as a prodigal son, ready to save his country from economic ruin. In 2001 he is forced to disclose that while living in Australia, he collected two convictions for possessing heroin, one in 1990 and the other in 1994. Each conviction carried a fine that was more appropriate for someone who had been dealing rather than simply using the drug. His public relations people dismiss this misdemeanour as 'a young man sowing his wild oats', practically patting him on the back. "I'm no worse than George Bush," says the suave Chief Executive in his defence, "look what he got up to when he was young."

In February 2000 during an exceptionally snowy winter, the tailings lake at the Australian mine at Baia Sprie, five kilometres from Baia Mare in the Maramureș, fills to overflowing with snow-thaw, bursts its sides and leaks into the Someș River. The Someș flows into Hungary, where it joins the River Tisa; the Tisa eventually meets the Danube. The leakage contains thousands of gallons of cyanide waste. Millions of fish die. Our television news reports show Hungarian fishermen holding the dead bodies and blaming Romania. The country's moral stock plummets again. Cyanide and toxic metals have seeped into the agricultural land around Baia Mare; local farmers will suffer for years to come, but after the fuss has died down, the world appears to care little for them.

A message to the London Guardian triggers a quick response; on 23 February John Vidal publishes a short paragraph about the worries over the environmental impact which the proposed Roșia Montana quarry will have. In April I manage to persuade the Canadian National Post to publish a piece as well; it is written by Keith Damsell who takes the trouble not only to ring me but Frankie too. The company's shares fall, and Frankie receives an abusive phone call from the mining company's boss in the middle of the night.

The French archaeologist presses home her advantage; before Baia Mare, the mining company would not talk to her, Frankie, nor any of us who were concerned about the impact of the mine on Roșia's heritage. As soon as she reaches an agreement with the company for some sort of survey and a museum, believing that saving something is better than nothing, the French archaeologist loses interest in the campaign. Initially she does her job well: she is involved in talks with the Romanian Ministry of Culture and the mining company. She writes an excellent report prefiguring what she would like to see done, but its contents are kept secret. Privately she tells Frankie that these are the best preserved and most sophisticated Roman mines ever discovered in Europe.

Before they can start the 'rescue archaeology', she and Frankie have to sign a contract with the company and the Ministry. The contract contains a confidentiality clause. Despite his concerns, Frankie is implicated; he relies on his job at the museum to support his family, he needs the money that is on offer. But to comply with the 'authorities' he must write no more critical articles. In contrast to the French archaeologist, Frankie is kept at arms' length by the Ministry and by the company; he is demoted from an important national archaeological committee. All this even though he is responsible for the county's archaeological heritage and it was he who introduced the French to the scene. He has made himself unpopular by sticking his neck out in public; local newspapers have listened to his fears and acted swiftly. But the 'big guys', the journalists in Bucharest, take no notice. After all, in 1990s Romania the catchphrase is 'investment, investment, investment': how else can the country hope to catch up with the rest of the world?

In July and September 2002 I return to Roşia Montana again. The July visit is for a Greenpeace protest. In the morning before I arrive, one of the company officials tries to start a fight between the pros and antis. A group of protesters have been standing together in the main square with their banners unfurled. Some miners from Roşia have walked over to them, shoved them about a bit and knocked their banners to the ground. Stephanie, the campaign coordinator, gets straight on the phone to the mining company's office, asking for the project manager.

"We had a gentleman's agreement," she says in her most measured and friendly tones, "and you are breaking it." He is shamed into action; the moment is over and things calm down.

Police with batons are out in force, big, burly men line the route of the protest from Zeno Cornea's mountainside meadow, complete with haystacks, along the mile or so of farm track that leads into the main square. Our part of the gentleman's agreement is to keep the main part of the protest out of sight. Four trestle tables end to end make an impromptu stage for the speakers. They move all of us by their passion; even the nationalistic Avram Iancu society, named after a 19th century Romanian patriot. We march peaceably into town. We have painted our banners the previous day, using materials provided by a contingent of fifteen activists from Greenpeace in Vienna and Budapest. They say: 'Nu transfor-

măm cer in iad' (Don't turn heaven into hell), 'Nu violaţi munţii noş-
tri' (Don't rape our mountains), 'Cyanide = death', and other pertinent messages.

At the end of the speeches, the resolutions, the collecting of
signatures and the march, we disperse. About four hundred people
from Roşia Montana and the villages of Corna and Bucium have
turned up, as well as some Romanian students from Constanţa on
the Black Sea coast and Baia Mare. It has felt more like a picnic
than a protest, and I am cheered by this coming together of so many
good minds. In the background the stark fact of the existing quarry
has confronted us all day long. On the other side of the valley, close
enough to hold a shouted conversation with anyone standing there,
there is a bleak, buff-coloured blankness, ugly and sterile, a gash in
the landscape, a promise of doom. Time seems very short indeed.

Sitting with us in the meadow listening to the cogent arguments are three young miners from Petroşani in the Jiu Valley. Two
years ago they bought a holiday home in Bucium Poieni. Their ban-
ner is the most provocative of all: it tells the company boss to get
lost, but in words that are less polite. It seems incredible: they are
miners and they are against the quarry.

It is a falsehood that environmentally-friendly alternatives to
modern living are a luxury, only available to countries that are already rich. The fact is none of us can afford to be without them.
This is what I have learnt from travelling in Romania if nothing else.

My second visit comes in September; I hire a 4 x 4 truck and
a driver for the day and go to Roşia from Bucium Poieni. The driver
is, I suspect, working for the mining company, but he cannot be
blamed for that; he has a wife and a baby son to support. I remember his wife. She had shouted at Françoise and the rest of us when
we tried to persuade her to join the July protest. "You will all
starve," she had said. She could be in her late twenties, but her features are drawn, and the little boy has a sickly face. Her husband is
happy to accept my offer of cash, which is far more than the going
rate.

I am glad to be riding in his inconspicuous Aro with its local
plates. Several times, journalists and visitors have been turned
away at the junction where you turn off to drive the last five kilometres into Roşia Montana. They were stopped by policemen in
trucks bearing the company's logo. The sense of tension rises as we
make our way into the town's main street. It could be my imagination; after all groups of teenagers are walking together down the
road, they look perfectly happy and pleased with themselves: maybe
their parents have accepted a cash offer, maybe they are in love.
Life goes on even here. I notice some of the houses which have been
sold; a blue and yellow plaque with the company logo has been

nailed to each one stating that it is now the property of Goldigger. A neat piece of psychological propaganda. As I stop to take a photo, a door in a neighbouring cottage opens a fraction, a man with a malicious expression looks round it. He watches me, but when I turn to stare back at him, he vanishes with a grimace.

"Are you going to the company office?" asks the driver.

"No, no," I say, startled by what is after all a reasonable question.

"Too many lies, is that it?" he suggests.

Someone has been undermining the land belonging to private properties: one or two gardens stand on the edge of a pit near the entrance to Catalina-Monuleşti, the gallery in which many of the wax tablets were found all those years ago. The land collapsed because someone was ferreting about in the ancient mine underneath. They had no legal right to be there. We stop outside one of the gardens, noticing the sunken flower beds. Its owner comes to meet us; it is Sanda, secretary and treasurer of Roşia Montana's own campaign group, Asociaţia Alburnus Maior. Sanda welcomes us with open arms: she treats the driver like a son and gives him and me a slap-up meal in her tiny, over-heated parlour.

Another member of the Alburnus Maior committee comes round; his name is Zeno. Zeno guides us to an entrance in the existing quarry, which is a mass of muddy hillsides connected by tracks wide enough for caterpillar earth-movers and interspersed with isolated sections of pasture and coppiced woodland. We are looking for Roman remains, and the places where there were Roman remains until the bulldozers pushed them flat. Walls and roads have vanished in the last eighteen months as though to deny the true importance of the site. Everywhere where there is still grass or trees there are tell-tale bumps in the ground: this time we know for a certainty that they belong to the Roman town - they must do: what other explanation is there? Present day Roşia Montana occupies a fraction of the area once covered by the Roman settlement.

Above us outlined against the skyline rise the jagged broken teeth of rocks, in which you can still see the neatly squared-off bores which the Roman engineers made two thousand years ago; we clamber up two of them, risking broken necks on the slippery cliff faces. Even the driver is impressed:

"I have never seen anything like this in my life," he tells us. We slip and slide knee deep across the ruts made by bulldozers to two other hills, where the remains of the pasture-covered land survives in its autumn colours, yet to be turned into pits and slag heaps. The driver stays behind; his shoes are not up to this. On the other side of a shallow comb is a copse; beyond this, on the sloping hillside, are the vestiges of a mausoleum. The walls were uncovered earlier in the year.

If it had not been for Zeno and the other campaigners the remains of the mausoleum might well have been destroyed. But they have taken photographs and videos and the pictures have been published in the Romanian papers. The mausoleum is a very unusual circular building, constructed of beautifully-shaped ashlar blocks linked with swallow-tail clamps as in the old Greek and Dacian way. The walls only come to knee height, but imagination can supply enough of the missing picture to show how fine a place it must have been. The mausoleum contains two graves. We do not know who they were designed for but the owners must have been rich and influential people, part of the wealthy society that developed in Alburnus Major thanks to its gold. How ironic that sounds today.

While I am trying to absorb all this, the tranquillity of the place is ruined by harsh voices yelling at us from the valley floor. We have been seen.

"You have no right to be here" says an aggressive, red-faced little woman, panting up the hill towards us in dungarees and a bobble hat. She is carrying a pickaxe; so is her rat-faced companion. They are locals whom the company has employed to keep an eye on the archaeological site; the quarry has been shut down for the winter and the archaeologists say they have completed their work.

Zeno takes the situation in hand; he is a natural rhetorician and demands to know why he, a native of Roşia Montana, should not visit a piece of his own heritage. He sows doubt in their minds as to the honesty and efficacy of the mining company's plans.

"I don't know who to believe," whines the woman. Despite herself she warms to Zeno's eloquence, and we reach a narrow plateau where everything teeters between good humour and violence. Treading carefully, we leave.

On the way back to Bucium the driver seems friendlier and more reflective.

"They cannot come here", he says, meaning the bulldozers and Bucium. He is half questioning, as though hoping for a reassuring negative.

The legal issues over who has the right to exploit the land here have not been resolved, at least not to Alburnus Maior's satisfaction. Other matters are being fought out, some losing ground, some gaining: the technicalities of mining economics, the question of an environmental licence, the legality or otherwise of moving people from their homes. Towering over these is the question of human rights and of the destruction of an irreplaceable piece of the world's heritage. At the worst moments, it seems that everything will come down to money. Whose money and how much we can only guess. The stakes are high, high enough for very dirty deals. It is the sheer, bare-faced affrontery that gets me. If this were part of western Europe, it could not happen. There is no justice: the company chairman who wants to make millions out of Roşia Montana was born in the Maramureş.

There is much more to say about the individual battles in the little-known war we are waging. There is the odd amusing skirmish, such as when a paper reports that the company is really after the Dacian's lost gold, or that a redundant miner has been caught blasting his way through some old galleries in the hope of getting rich. As I leave this account, the struggle continues; in some ways it is getting nastier. The gold price has been fluttering up again in the past twelve months, making technical opposition to the scheme less credible. But the long-term social, economic, environmental and cultural arguments against the quarry are as cogent as ever. For how much longer the pleasant mountains of Roşia Montana and Bucium will stand, giving identity and proportion to people's lives, is still anybody's guess.

> Taci codre! nu mă-ntreaba
> Ce-am pierdut nu pot afla
> C-am pierdut o ruja plină
> Şi pă mândra din inima...

> ('Quiet forest, do not ask me
> What I've lost cannot be found
> I have lost a full sweet rose
> And my lover from my heart...)

Romanians love to sing sad songs like this, but during my search for Sarmizegetusa, which is far from over yet, I have met many people who contradict the melancholy sentiments which the 'doina' expresses. The people who have impressed me and given me the most hope for Romania's future are the country's young greens who want to create sustainable alternatives to global consumerism. They are not infantile or hysterical, but determined and intelligent people who can see beyond the end of their next pay cheque.

There are those such as Stephanie, who came to Roşia Montana hotfoot from another successful environmental campaign in Romania. She took up verbal arms against Goldigger in April 2002; at the time of writing she is still there. A central European with a ready wit, Stephanie has endeared herself to the villagers. Her honesty gives them something to cling to in the morass of half-truths and false promises. She appears at important local events clad in her "lucky" trousers, faded pink tracksuit bottoms that look like baggy Turkish shalwar.

Then there is Teodora, who is helping to develop a sustainable, alternative plan for the valleys. She began as a shy volunteer ecologist and now runs Ecotopia Romania. Close to Stephanie is Stefania, who works for the Cluj-based non-governmental organisation, PATRIR, standing for Institutul Român pentru Acțiune, Instruire și Cercetare in Domeniul Păcii (The Romanian Institute for Action, Instruction and Research into Peace). One of the most energetic groups involved is the Cluj Cyclo-touring Club. There are many others, men and women, Romanians and foreigners, who turned up in person or via e-mail and the internet. They were mostly young people in their teens and twenties, energetic, cool and passionate at the same time, with a real vision for the future. It has been a privilege to meet them.

Appendix

1. Note on Pronunciation

Sarmizegetusa has six syllables and in English sounds something like this, Sarm-*ee*-zay-jet-*oo*-za,with the emphasis on the syllables in bold italics.

Romanian is a Latin language in which words are pronounced more or less as they look, but there are a number of accents that change how letters sound. The easiest to say are the character ş which sounds like the English "sh", and the ă which sounds like "er". Then there is ţ which makes an ordinary t into "ts".

The hardest accents are the â and î which come from Slavonic and are virtually interchangeable. I have used "uh" as the English equivalent, but it is difficult to reproduce this sound accurately without hearing it spoken. It turns the word "câine", which means dog, into something like "cuh*ee*nay", with the â very short as though you are swallowing it.

C followed by e or i is always soft, like the English "ch" in cheese; whilst in Romanian "ch" is hard as in the English k, so that chip (face) sounds like "keep". G reacts the same way with an e or an i after it, and gh is hard as in the man's name Gheorghe (Gay*or*gay).

Usually when there is an i at the end of a Romanian word, it is left silent, as in Deseşti, which is pronounced Day-s*e*sht, or Bucureşti (Boocoo-rr*e*sht) with a lovely rolling of the r. Romanians often ellide "ea" so that you can hardly hear the two letters separately.

In Romanian, a typical greeting goes like this: Buna dimineaţa (Boona dimini*a*tsa, Good morning), Ce mai faceţi (Che mai f*a*chets; how are you?); if the person you are talking to does not understand what you have said, they might reply, Poftim? (Pofft*ee*m? What did you say? or How can I help you?) or Ce anume? (Che an*oo*meh? What was that?) Goodbye is La revedere (La reved*e*reh) which means the same as the Italian Arrivederci; friends might kiss each other on both cheeks and then say Te pup, pa pa (which sounds rather like Toad in the Wind the Willows: Teh poop, pah pah, and means Kiss kiss, bye bye).

2. Glossary of terms

Akathist: literally this means "sung while standing" and it refers to the hymns which early Orthodox monks wrote in celebration of the saints. The most famous Akathist is the one composed by Romanos the Syrian for the Virgin Mary in the 6th century. It had 24 verses and is performed in many Romanian monasteries on Fridays and special feast days. In the 16th century the 24 verses of the Marian Akathist were translated into a series of frescoes on the outer walls of the painted churches of Bucovina.

Exarchate of Peri: an exarchate is a term used by the Orthodox Church for a monastery that lies far away from the Patriarchate in Constantinople; the exarch was an archbishop whom the Patriarch charged with a special mission, in this case to train his own monks.

Frate: the word for a monk in the Romanian Orthodox Church; it means Brother.

Imperial Doors: the two central doors of the icon screen which are opened during Church services. Behind them is the sanctuary containing the altar. The only people allowed to pass through the doors are the officiating priests.

Maica: this is the word for nun in the Romanian Orthodox Church; it means Mother or Sister;

Monastery: In the Orthodox Church, a "monastery" can be managed by monks or nuns; there is no equivalent for the word "convent".

3. Some books and web addresses

Friedrich Teja Bach et al: *Constantin Brâncuşi* (Philadelphia Mus. of Art, 1995)

Paul Bailey: *Kitty and Virgil* (Fourth Estate, 1998)

Marcu Beza: *The Romanian Church* (SPCK, 1943)

Lucian Boia: *Romania: a European borderland* (Reaktion Books, 2001)

Barbu Brezianu: *Brâncuşi in Romania* (Editura ALL, 1999)

Alan Brownjohn: *Long Shadows* (Dewi Lewis, Stockport, 1997)

Ana Burca/Dan Dinescu: *The Wooden Architecture of Maramureş* (Humanitas, 1997)

Dennis Deletant: *Romania under Communist Rule* (The Center for Romanian Studies, 1999)

Jessica Douglas-Home: *Once Upon Another Time* (Michael Russell, 2000)

Richard Douthwaite: *Short Circuit: strengthening local economies for security in an unstable world* (The Lilliput Press, 1996)

Mircea Eliade: *The Romanians: a Concise History* (Editura Roza Vintorilor, 1992)

Marija Gimbutas: *The Civilization of the Goddess* (Harper, San Francisco. 1991)

Misha Glenny: *The Rebirth of History* (Penguin, 1993)

Vesna Goldsworthy: *Inventing Ruritania* (Yale University Press, 1998)

Keith Hitchins: *Rumania 1866-1947* (Clarendon Press, 1994)

Gail Kligman: *The Wedding of the Dead* (California University Press, 1986)

Patrick Leigh Fermor: *Between the Woods and the Water* (John Murray, 1998)

Naomi Mitchison: *The Corn King and the Spring Queen* (Cannongate, 1990)

Kosei Miya: *La Roumanie des Quatre Saisons* (Musee de l'Homme, Paris, 1997)

James Roberts: *Guide to the Mountains of Romania* (Cicerone, 1999)

Romanian Young Nature Friends, ed.: *Între Cer şi Pământ (Between Sky and Earth), an anthology of essays* (Editura Brumar, Timişoara, 2000)

Joseph Rothschild and Nancy M. Wingfield: *Return to Diversity: a Political History of East Central Europe since World War II* (Oxford University Press, 2000)

Kurt Treptow (ed.): *A History of Romania* (The Center for Romanian Studies, 1996)

Katherine Verdery: *Transylvanian Villagers* (University of California Press, 1983)

Timothy Ware (Bishop Kallistos): *The Orthodox Church* (Penguin, 1993)

***

Ecotopia Romania: http://ecotopia.ngo.ro

The Roşia Montana campaign website: www.rosiamontana.org

Lucy Castle's website: www.lucycastle.co.uk

Între Cer şi Pământ: www.banat.ro/tpn

The Romanian Crafts Foundation: www.crafts.go.ro.com